IN THE SHADE OF THE MAPLE TREE

Dialogues with St. Padre Pio

Orest Stocco

IN THE SHADE OF THE MAPLE TREE

Copyright © 2015 by Orest Stocco

ISBN 978-1-926442-06-8

Edited by Penny Lynn Cates

Cover Design by Penny Lynn Cates

ALSO BY OREST STOCCO

NOVELS

The Golden Seed
Tea with Grace
Jesus Wears Dockers
Healing with Padre Pio
Keeper of the Flame
My Unborn Child
On the Wings of Habitat
What Would I Say Today If I Were to Die Tomorrow?

NON FICTION

The Lion that Swallowed Hemingway
The Sum of All Spiritual Paths
Do We Have An Immortal Soul?
Stupidity Is Not a Gift of God
Letters to Padre Pio
Old Whore Life
Just Going with the Flow
Why Bother? The Riddle of the Good Samaritan
The Pearl of Great Price

A Note from the Author

I'm not a psychic. I'm a creative writer. And the following dialogues with St. Padre Pio are an exercise in active imagination.

This is a technique that the eminent Swiss psychologist C. G. Jung introduced to the world with his journey of self-discovery, which he recorded in his journals that he later transcribed into *The Red Book*; but there is nothing new about active imagination. Creative writers do it all the time.

Active imagination is a dialogue with the unconscious. It is more than a dialogue, actually; it is a dialectical exercise in reconciling the unconscious with the conscious self. A novelist, for example, engages his unconscious to produce the images that he needs to reconcile elements of his unconscious with his conscious self; just as Neale Donald Walsch did with his *Conversations with God* series of books. He engaged his unconscious to resolve personal issues, and his unconscious spoke to him by way of the God image.

The image that I engaged in for this book of dialogues was the Ascended Master St. Padre Pio. I had a relationship with him for my novel *Healing with Padre Pio*, which was based on ten sessions that I had with a psychic who communicated with Saint Padre Pio; but I can make no claim that it was the spirit of Padre Pio that came through in my dialogues just as Neale Donald Walsch can make no claim that it was God that spoke to him. It is all subjective.

Nonetheless, I enjoyed my dialogues with the Good Saint; not simply because they stretched my creative muscles, but because of what came through in our dialogues. It was a healing experience.

Orest Stocco,
Georgian Bay, Ontario
August 21, 2014

Table of Contents

1. In the Shade of the Maple Tree

Saturday, June 28, 2014

"Good morning, Padre. Imagine us sitting in a chair under the maple tree in my front yard this early morning with the birds just beginning their morning chirping and we are enjoying a fresh cup of coffee waiting for the sun to rise above the tree line and we engage in a gentle talk as the spirit of this creative exercise in active imagination moves us...

"Well, I brought my novel *The Golden Seed* to closure. I had no idea how it was going to end, but it came to closure on its own; and it completely surprised me, because the ending brought the story full-circle. So, thank you Padre. I asked you in my last letter to help me bring closure to my novel, and I could not have asked for a better ending."

"*First things first. Good morning, my friend. And yes, by all means let us engage in a gentle talk and see where the spirit of our dialogues takes us. Now; you're welcome. I enjoyed your new book. It is one of your best creative efforts, and it promises to have a long shelf life. It needs to be out as soon as possible, because there is a need for this kind of fiction. Do everything you can to get a publisher for this one. By all means, work on publishing it yourself; but work all the angles for this book. It is special.*"

"In what way special?"

"*The fantasy of returning to a decision will enlighten the reader on how to choose correctly the first time around. Time is of no importance in the realm of soul, and a decision made today can be changed tomorrow in another world, for such is the multi-dimensionality of soul. This is a concept of parallel worlds that is being introduced to the world today, and The Golden Seed is an entry point into this reality. As you have come to believe, literature does have an effect on life; that's what brings light to the human condition.*"

"I don't suppose you can give me anything specific on where I should send *The Golden Seed*?"

"*You must do your own research. It is the law of spiritual growth.*"

"But why the nudges, then? Isn't that intervening?"

"*Yes. But that's a very complicated question. Intervention without interfering does not violate the principle of spiritual growth because it leaves it open for you to decide. You are merely nudged.*"

"What do you think of my book *The Lion that Swallowed Hemingway*?"

"*It is very informative. It will do much better than you anticipate, once it finds its proper place in the pantheon of Hemingway literature.*"

"I have a feeling that I should send a copy of this book to a number of people. I need not mention them here, but what do you think of this idea?"

"*This is how it will find its way into the pantheon of Hemingway literature. The author of Hemingway's Boat would appreciate it.*"

"On a personal note, this money situation. Penny's in a quandary again, and when she's in a quandary so am I. Will this ever resolve itself?"

"*Yes, yes, yes! Do not fret. The door has been opened. Tomorrow will bring new hope, new love, and new happiness. I promise you.*"

"Padre, I've come a long way since my novel *Healing with Padre Pio*. I've written half a dozen books since, and I think I understand you now when you said that I have transcended my own voice; but I feel alienated now. I just don't seem to fit in anywhere. I'm so out of context with life that I feel like an alien. Is this what happens to anyone that transcends their own voice?"

"*Not necessarily, but often it is the case. When you transcend your own voice you speak from a higher perspective. This perspective is beyond the reach of most people, though highly recognizable; this is what makes one so puzzling. They can be*" *heard and understood, but not really; they are perceived to be different but the same, and this paradox is hard on the psyche. That's why you feel the gap between yourself and the rest of the world. I began to experience this shortly after I received the blessing of the Holy Wounds. I was no longer the same as my fellow monks, but still the same person; and the difference set me apart for the rest of my life. Then it became more and more obvious as I grew in spiritual consciousness. Your growth in spiritual consciousness far exceeds the growth of the average person. You excel in your growth because of your writing, which opens you up to more and more spiritual growth. It is your way to the selfless self. This is why you keep transcending yourself."*

"Can I trust my own mind?"

"No. The mind will always look for a way to keep you from transcending yourself. It is to the nature of the mental world to keep you there."

"We're going to get our driveway paved. I see this as a symbolic paving of our life—the paving of the way for us. What do you think?"

"Your understanding of the symbolic language of life is as close to the truth as it can get. Yes, the paving of your life has begun, and when your driveway has been paved the way will be much clearer for you and your loved one. Trust in the goodness of your own nature. Your life has taken you to the edge of the greatest mystery, and you are about to enter into a world of wonder like you have never seen before."

"No hyperbole, please. I'm still very vulnerable when it comes to my ego, despite how conscious I may be of my foolish expectations."

"One is a fool who does not work for his dreams. You work for your dreams, and they have to manifest one day; that is the law of balance. Input equals output. It is inevitable."

"I hope I'm around to see it!"

"You will be. You are. It is happening now. The process of your new life in the wonder of your dreams has begun to unfold with the

paving of your driveway. It is much more symbolic than you imagine!"

"What do you think of the idea of sending a chapter of *The Golden Seed* to a Canadian publisher?"

"It may surprise you."

"I may do that this morning. So what do you say we bring this short talk under the maple tree to closure on that note?"

"Excellent note to end it on. Have a wonderful day, my good friend. Until we talk again..."

2. Dare to Take the Plunge?

Sunday, June 29, 2014

"Good morning, Padre. I hesitate, but I'm nudged to take the plunge. You know what plunge I mean—into this process of active imagination, which would be this dialogue with you that I can simply refer to as a Soul talk, something like my Soul talk books in which I let go and let the creative unconscious speak, only in this case YOU are the focus of my attention and the voice of my creative unconscious. Is this too bold?"

"No. It is an exercise in creative expression. Try it and see where it goes. I'm game if you are."

"Isn't that how Neale Donald Walsch started, by writing God an angry letter to get all that stuff off his chest?"

"Yes. He opened himself up to what you call the 'creative unconscious.'"

"What do you call it?"

"I call it Soul. Soul is who you are. Soul is who we all are; but, as you have so diligently worked it out in your own books, the individuation of Soul is what the process of life is all about. Of all the writers on this subject, few have given this process the clarity that you have. It is an expression of the journey of the unconscious self to the conscious self and on to the spiritually self-realized self. That is what life is all about, and your dialogues with me are an expression of this journey in the widest possible context. Take the plunge."

"In all frankness, I hesitate to take this plunge because I'm afraid of the delusional aspects of my own mind. I can't trust the egoic factor of the mind. It is forever seeking attention and adulation and is easily inflated because it can never get enough of itself. It is always grasping for attention, and it creates all kinds of scenarios to focus the eyes of the world upon itself. This is ego's great virtue, because it drives the individuation of our spiritual self; but it is also ego's greatest weakness, because it traps Soul in an unreal world. Ego can get so lost in this world of make-believe that it can destroy one's life, as Ernest Hemingway found out. He got lost in his own delusions and the pressure was too much and he took his own life. So, to plunge or not to plunge?"

"All good points, and worth considering; but you have come a long way from the days when you abandoned to the creative process in your lonely little apartment in Annecy, France. You were a tortured and mixed-up soul then, but you have journeyed a long way since. You have climbed out of your Platonic cave and have seen the light of Divine Spirit. You are free to take the plunge if you so desire. I will neither encourage nor discourage you; but I can assure you that this is only an exercise in active imagination. Try to imagine the horror that Doctor Jung must have felt when he let the bottom drop out of his life and plunged into the depths of his own unconscious; but he did it, and his Red Book is one of the greatest living chronicles of one man's search for his lost soul. As trite as it may sound, nothing ventured nothing gained."

"You don't mince words. I like that. What bothered me with all of my 'dialoguing' in Annecy, France—a strange form of automatic writing!—was that I never got any information that I could verify. It was all pabulum for my ego; nothing nutritious for my soul. All it did was keep me stuck in Plato's cave. It did nothing to unfetter me from my fantasy-making ego self."

"True; but it was a process that gave you a background to compare the real thing with. When you did connect with your creative self in your writing you could see the difference between the empty world of your fantasies and the real world of creative expression. The former is made up of pure mind stuff, while the latter is made up of the real and imagined. That is the difference."

"Fair enough. But what I'm really asking is this: how can I be sure that I am dialoguing with you and not my own mind?"

"Only time will tell."

"Okay, let's say that I take the plunge and pursue this mode of creative expression, which I'd simply call 'Soul Talks with

Padre Pio,' are you saying that in time the nature of our Soul talks will define itself?"

"Yes. Just as every one of your books found its own way, so will our talks find their own way; so, begin by initiating a dialogue—"

"Let's talk about this notion of transcending my own voice. You told me that I had transcended my voice and the voice of my spiritual community, and by that I took you to mean that I no longer spoke from my personality but from my higher self. Am I correct in this understanding?"

"Yes. You shifted your center of gravity from your evolving self to your evolved self; that is what made the difference. Once you centered yourself in your evolved self, you spoke from the totality of your evolved self. This is the difference between the person stuck in Plato's cave and the person who has been liberated from Plato's cave. The light is much better outside the cave, and reality is much clearer. The transcendent self is one's true self."

"Being one's transcendent self doesn't mean that one is in a state of total consciousness, does it? Because I don't feel that I am. I do feel however that when I know something, I know it; I don't just understand it, I know it without doubt. It is a kind of gnostic knowing that needs no confirmation. Is this what it means to be one's transcendent self, when what one has experienced in his life, and all of his lives, becomes his reality, his truth?"

"Precisely. One's transcendent self is one's true self. It is the evolved individuated truth of all of one's personalities on earth. It is the essential reality of his being, which does not mean, as you say, that one is privy to the Being of all beings; but it is the entry point into the Oneness of God."

"What is the point of all of this, if you don't mind?"

"To get you to see the reality of your own nature; to get you to appreciate what you have become; to get you to stop doubting yourself."

"The weaning of my soul—"

"Yes."

"I beg you to have patience with me, then."

7

"And love and compassion and all that comes with the job of being a guardian of the sacred wisdom. I am privileged to be working with you in the development of your talent. You have realized a gift that will bring much light to the world. You simply do not have the objectivity to see it yet. But one day, and before you leave your mortal coil, you will see it. I promise you."

"It would be nice, but I'm not hanging my hat on it—"

"Good answer. On that note, have a wonderful day; and remember: live, love, and enjoy your life. And don't worry about tomorrow, because tomorrow never comes. There is only today."

"Yeah, right!"

3. Well?

Thursday, July 5, 2014

"Good morning, Padre. Well? I've just added the table of contents to my second volume of letters to you, which I've called *The Sum of All Spiritual Paths*, and I'm curious to know what you think of my new book."

"*I love the title. And you are correct in your interpretation, because the self is the sum of all spiritual paths once one has made the connection with the inner self, which is what the journey through life is all about. So all paths are necessary to get to the inner self, but when one makes the connection with the inner self then one must live one's own life, which is now the sum of all spiritual paths. Don't wait too long to get it out. It's a catchy title, and it might just capture the attention of the reader in search of answers.*"

"There are a lot of those out there, but it's been my experience that most seekers aren't serious; or, rather, they can only go so far before they faint out. Why this is so has intrigued me for a long time. After a lot of thought, it was Carl Jung who supplied the answer that I was looking for: understanding devours one's soul, if I can express it this way; and people don't want to be devoured. That's why they can only go so far in their search for truth—they don't want the truth to devour them. Do you see what I mean?"

"*Certainly. This is one of your most insightful moments, thanks to your need to find the answer. It's because of your need to know that keeps the merciful law of synchronicity, as you call the Love of God, active in your life; and in your discovery, you enrich the consciousness of life.*"

"I'm reminded of what Jung said about the high-blown language of the archetype; so, please, let's keep it humble. I don't need any stroking!"

"Fair enough. But whether I'm an archetype or the voice of your fellow companion is open to question. In time, you will come to your own realization. This is a new chapter in your life. It will prove to be interesting in ways that you cannot imagine, because when one engages Spirit in dialogue one never knows where Spirit will take one—"

"Fair enough. Being one with Spirit, archetype or not, our dialogue will go where it will, for such is the way of the creative unconscious—"

"Not so. The creative unconscious speaks for the individual self, not Spirit as such; there is a distinction, which you should correct in your opening remarks to your reader in The Sum of All Spiritual Paths.*"*

"What is this distinction? Is that like the light shining through a spectrum with the self being the spectrum?"

"Well put. When you and Penny were talking you used the metaphor of a diamond. The self is like a diamond that refracts the light of Spirit. The creative unconscious is the creative energy that is refracted through the unrealized Self, and I use the word Self with a capital S because this speaks to the 'I' of God that is always in a state of unfoldment."

"Pardon me while I go back to my book to make my correction. I'll be back shortly...Okay, I've made my correction. Is that better?"

"YES. This distinction is necessary to appreciate the unfolding self in conjunction with the unfolding Self. This is the mystery of the self."

"Alright. This opens up the big question that has been nagging me for quite some time now: the kink in the spiritual paths of life. They all seem to put the carriage in front of the horse, in one way or another. Am I wrong in my perception? Or am I just venting some residual anger?"

"You're not wrong, and yes; you are still venting residual anger. But that's okay. You have to get it out of your system. The spiritual life is a very tricky thing to get a hold of. The world is still so young, and it will take a long time before the world sees that it must put the horse in front of the carriage. As you say, man is God-dependent, and the great shift in social consciousness is all about coming to the realization that man is ultimately responsible for the way the world is unfolding. We and the world are one. We are the world. But this is a very hard truth to shoulder. It scares people. This is why there's so much confusion in the world today. People are running scared. The mere thought of shouldering the world's responsibility is enough to scare even the boldest of saints—myself included!"

"So what's the answer?"

"Just live your life and let God take care of the rest. That's all we can do. We have no choice but to trust in the Infinite."

"I suspect that this is the effect that my writing has upon the reader's consciousness—it foreshadows this enormous responsibility, and they flee in horror. Am I right?"

"To a point. The biggest factor has to do with not wanting to give one credit for one's growth and accomplishments. That's human nature. One doesn't have to know you personally to dismiss you; one can be a stranger and see in you what they don't want to acknowledge. They know they should, but they cannot bring themselves to acknowledge what your writing awakens in them. But that is about to change once you break the ice. Remember your dream years ago of the ice field that cracked under your feet? That's happening now. Just keep writing and get your books out there. The Love of God will take care of you."

"It all comes down to trust, doesn't it?"

"Yes. But trust is not an easy virtue. It took me most of my life to learn how to trust God."

"You're going to tell me your secret, aren't you?"

"No secret. God wore me down, that's all. I could no longer not trust God. I was brought to that place where either I trusted God or I did not trust God, and I could not throw my life out the

window; so I surrendered and embraced God heart and soul. That's the secret if you want to call it a secret."

"I can hear you laughing. I'm still looking for the magic formula, and I don't think I will ever stop; but the magic formula is in the DOING!"

"Yes. In DOING, you ARE. That's the magic formula. It's always been that way. That's the sum of all spiritual paths—but learn to love what you DO. And if you are fortunate enough to find something that you love to do, that's even better; because that makes DOING fun."

"Padre, I've exhausted my creative energies for writing. I've got a little job to do on our driveway. They're coming tomorrow to prep it for paving, and I can't wait because I see the paving of our driveway as a symbol for the paving of our life, and God, I hope I'm right! So, thanks for the chat."

"You're welcome."

4. Woe Is Me

Wednesday, July 9, 2014

"Good morning, Padre. It's happening again, that woe is me feeling that seems to kick in whenever I finish a new book, that downward spiral when the well is empty and I feel like I have no purpose and everything seems to take on much more significance than before and it seems like the whole world wants to crash in on me and I want to crawl into a hole and die; so I thought I'd have a little talk with you hoping you might lift up my spirits."

"The days are long when you are not writing. Writing is your way of staying connected to the creative energy of life; so, write!"

"I understand the logic, but there's the discouragement of not seeing the benefits of my writing, other than seeing my writing in book form; it just seems so long to get myself out there. You did tell me that after three years something would begin to happen..."

"The effect of your writing is working on the psyche of the world in its own way, and it is happening on a level beyond your imagination; but I assure you, you are making a difference to the evolution of social consciousness."

"Padre, I'm tired. Physically, emotionally, mentally, and spiritually; I'm tired, and I look forward to crossing over—but I don't want to leave Penny. I do hope I go first, though. I couldn't do without her if she left me. I'd die!"

"As you say, she is your life."

"Thank you for my spiritual healing. I never thought that I was as vain as I was until I met you, and were it not for the ten spiritual sessions that I had with you I don't know where I would be today. Can you tell me, out of curiosity; because it would fascinate me to know?"

"You would still be struggling with the issue. Vanity is the last to go on Soul's' journey home to God. You were blessed to experience what you did, and the results have been remarkable. Your writing is now free of the conceit that mars the literature of so many writers, including your model Hemingway. Once again, what keeps you from writing your stories? That is where your talent has taken you, and it would be foolish not to capitalize on your journey of the self."

"I dream of one day being as authentic as you. Is that ever going to happen before I cross over?"

"The answer lies in your writing. Through your writing you sculpt yourself and realize the gem of your own genius. Authenticity is a reality as long as you make it so, and the creative process is one of the best ways to sculpt yourself of all that disagrees with who you are. To be, you must do; and creative writing is your path to the authenticity that you seek."

"Am I going to rework those novels I just looked at—*The Waking Dream* and *Cathedral of My Past Lives*?"

"Those novels have already been published over here. You have to work on them to be published over there. The two worlds, though parallel realities, do exist independently of each other. This is something you have yet to learn."

"Why can't I dream of my life on the other side? Why do I keep going back to my life in my hometown? What the hell is blocking me from experiencing my life of writing in my dreams, my career in the literary world?"

"As I said, the two worlds are independent of each other. Why would you dream of a life that is already in progress? Your life over here is rich in what you would like your life there to be; but your duty in your current life is to make the life over here possible. This is the mystery of the self's journey."

"I don't know what to make of this. I could still have more exciting dreams, could I not? Why are my dreams so fatiguing?"

"The more fatiguing your dreams, the more progress you are making; that is the way of the dream. You grow in your dreams, whether you realize it or not. Your dreams give you the impetus to continue in your writing, your journey, your own growth in wholeness and singleness of self."

"I'm too tired to continue. I think I'm going to shave and go for a nice walk, or bike ride. Thanks. Until again..."

5. A Feeling of Dread

Thursday, July 10, 2014

"Good morning, Padre. I have this feeling of dread hanging over me, and I can't seem to shake it. It's not oppressive, as such; but I can feel it lurking, and I'd like to get rid of it. Has my past come back to haunt me?"

"Not as such. Your past is your past, and it has its own history; meaning, it has its beginning, middle, and end. This means that what happens, happens; and today is today. Don't let the ghosts of your past haunt you. The best way to keep them away is to live today. Do what you have to do today, and let the past fade into a memory. That's the way to live in the now."

"I feel like crying. I can't help it, but I just feel like crying. I know from the biographies that I read of your life that you cried an awful lot. You cried for Jesus' suffering and the suffering of the world. I feel like crying for no reason other than that I just feel like crying. Why?"

"Your heart has been opened much wider than you realize. You have been brought to that place in your life where you can join in the mysteries of human evolution. The mysteries of the deep are about to be revealed to you."

"The workings of the inner universe?"

"Yes. That's one way of putting it."

"I do have to be careful of inflation. I fell for that before, and I don't want to fall for that again. What are these mysteries of the deep? How am I going to learn, or experience them? What, no response?"

"It is a very tricky situation. Your inner self wants to be realized, but your ego still has influence over what comes out, filtering it to satisfy itself; but you are well aware of the concept of

inflation, and that is as it should be. You want to cry for all the things that could have been. Everyone does."

"Why did you cry so much?"

"I identified with Christ's suffering. His suffering became mine, and it was real. My pain was real. My tears were real. That was my way."

"Padre, what is my way? I've come so far that I feel like I am all by myself in a land of no inhabitants. Where is everyone?"

"I am here. This is a land where the souls that have come to fruition in their own identity come. You are home, my child."

"Home? I don't feel like I'm home. I feel isolated and alone. Padre, why cannot I meet people of the same ilk? I'm reading Jung again, and I feel really good in his company as I'm reading about his life. But I felt better in your company when we had my spiritual healing sessions. I love the way you understood me, accepted me, and let me be me but all the while teaching me to continue on my journey of the heart. God, when I read some of my old stuff now how wretched I was in my vanity—"

"Not wretched. That's not the correct word. You were very conceited, that's a fact; but it was because of your conceit that you found me. Without it you would be still out there working your way through the tangled web of life. It will always be a tangled web, and there's nothing anyone can do about it. That's the nature of the enantiodromiac process; but you have extracted yourself. Now you are free of the tug and pull of life. That's why you are alone."

"Life really is a journey through vanity to humility, isn't it?"

"That is the best description that I have heard of the life experience. We have to grow in our vanity to grow spiritually. That's the process which you saw in the Book of Ecclesiastes. Yes, we will work together again. Do not fret about you economic circumstances. They are about to change."

"For the better or worse?"

"For the better. Your time is coming. Your writing has begun to break the field of ice. You are about to experience your life as a

writer as you have always wanted it to be. You are being followed and read."

"I'd like to believe that. Let's keep it humble, please. I don't want to feed on morsels of hope. I want to experience the reality of being. Do you think I can salvage my novel *The Waking Dream* from the wicked conceit of my inflated ego?"

"Yes. And because of your new perspective the story will take on the flavor that will make it a best seller. It will happen. Believe it!"

"I feel like a worm that has crawled out of a deep dark hole and am a worm no longer. I am a man that was a worm, and the memories of crawling out of the hole are pressing upon me. Is that it?"

"Pretty much. In my day, we called it feeling the depths of one's sinful life. I pretty much identify with how you feel. I felt worse."

"Will Penny and I ever have care-free days? You know the kind of days I mean, free of the anxiety that burdens us today?"

"Sooner than you think. Just keep writing and sending your books out. It's all in the cards. You have the winning hand, it has to be played."

"How? When?"

"Trust your instincts. Let your gut tell you what to do. Once the process starts, there's no stopping it..."

"Thank you."

6. My Jungian Dream

Monday, July 14, 2014

"Good morning, Padre. Penny finished editing my new novel *The Golden Seed* yesterday, and she loves it. 'It's fabulous. It's the best thing you've ever written,' she said. That meant the world to me, because Penny's opinion matters more than anyone's. I write because she has made it possible for me to write, and whatever success I achieve in writing it will be because of her; so I'm thrilled that she loves my new novel. What do you think of it?"

"I think it's one of your best works. I can't say that it is your best because I favour Healing with Padre Pio, for obvious reasons; but The Golden Seed will make its way around the world and find its place in the reader's heart. It is one of those books that transcends time and will be around as long as books are. You have a right to be proud of this novel."

"I'd like to share a dream I had the other night. It was what I can call a 'Jungian dream.' I say this because it spoke to me in Jungian language, the archetypal language of the unconscious. I was with some people in my dream, two men, one wearing an Australian type hat, a cowboy hat that has become distinctly Australian in its style, and the other man didn't have a hat but was dressed more like a city person, and he gave me the impression that he was an agent of sort, perhaps a literary agent, or a business representative, and there was someone else but he was invisible to me, but he had a jaguar on a leash; and the jaguar came up to me, extending its paw onto my arm, but it did not claw me even though it gave me a fright, and it stared into my face and opened its mouth and I heard a woman's voice coming from deep within the jaguar, and it spoke to me: 'Go into the forest and pick pine mushrooms.' And then the scene changed. I saw a woman, very smart looking, in her late forties or early fifties, dressed in what looked like safari clothes, and she had a large manila envelope, the kind that I used to mail out a manuscript, and the envelope was slit and it was raining and rain got into the envelop and I was worried that the words on the paper inside would get smudged, but she lifted the envelope and let the water pour out, and then she went away, presumably to mail or deliver it; and that was my dream. Now I'll give you my interpretation and then you can give me yours. The jaguar was my anima, the female side of my soul; and being on a leash told me that my anima has been tamed. I know the jaguar was my anima because of the woman's voice that spoke when the jaguar opened its mouth and the female voice spoke to me. She told me to go into the forest and pick pine mushrooms. I didn't know there was a mushroom by this name (I looked it up on Google later and found out that pine mushrooms do exist, and they are called by the Japanese name 'matsutake,' which are rare and very expensive mushrooms, even as much if not more than truffles), but I took 'pine mushrooms' to be a symbol for my creative writing, namely my short stories that I have started to write in my new book *Enantiodromia,* and I took 'forest' to be a symbol of my unconscious. So I took the dream to be my unconscious confirming what you told me long ago, that I should be writing the stories that I have been putting off all these years. My unconscious was giving me permission to write them, so I no longer have to doubt myself. What do you think?"

"I would agree. Your unconscious has confirmed where your writing should go, which your novel The Golden Seed will prepare the way for you to take because it will give you all the confidence you need to write creatively. That was a wonderful dream, and I concur with your interpretation."

"And the envelope?"

"That's your soul telling you to seek out a publisher for your 'pine mushrooms.' Now that you have completed your literary memoir (The Lion that Swallowed Hemingway) and have merged your two paths—your literary calling and your calling to find your true self—into one path of creative writing, you have no choice but

to heed the directive from your unconscious. Soul wants you to write stories. That is your path for the rest of your life."

"I've opened up my file and have begun to work my way back into my book of short stories, and I feel that's my next project; but I'm still called to write my spiritual musings and continue my dialogue with you."

"By all means, continue with your musings and our dialogue; that exercises a different set of creative muscles, and it will be very informative for your readers. You do have people who follow your spiritual musings, and your readership will flourish once your name gets out there."

"I think after Penny gets *The Golden Seed* out I'm going to give her my second volume of letters to you, called *The Sum of All Spiritual Paths*. I want that one out after *The Golden Seed*. What do you think?"

"I enjoyed that book of letters. Each letter was special to me, and I can't wait to see it in print. It will surprise you. The title will entice many readers and give you a whole new readership. Trust the process."

"Again, thank you..."

7. Here I go Again

Tuesday, July 15, 2014

"Good morning, Padre. I don't know what's going on. It feels like I'm sinking into a state of depression. I don't even know what to think about it. I've got to snap out of it. I can't do this to Penny. I need your help."

"Your lack of sleep contributes to this significantly. Sleep is a great healer of the day's concerns. You must teach yourself to sleep. Without the radio!"

"I'm scared. I haven't been this scared in a long time. I don't even want to open up the subject because it terrifies me."

"Understood. We won't open it up, then. We will talk about what you must do to get your life in order. You must walk every day. That is a priority. Walking will get you out into the fresh air and the exercise will refresh your muscles and limber you up and dissipate some of that negative energy that you take in with the radio every night while you sleep. You must stop listening to the radio when you go to bed. It is a bad habit and the cause of your moods. And you must teach yourself to drink at least six glasses of water daily. Your diet has to be restricted so you can lose a few pounds. It is necessary for your emotional health as well as your physical health. Rest properly."

"How?"

"Rest your mind. Don't think while you are resting. Let your mind drift into a state of no-thought. Just let go and let God."

"What about our daily concerns? How long must we endure this pressure of economic fear?"

"It won't last very long. It is on its way out. Please trust me."

"I so much want to, Padre; but what do I have to go on?"

"What you've always had—faith in yourself. You must take charge of your life. You must regain your sense of control. That's

the source of your woes. You feel that because of your health you have been losing control of your life, but what do you do about your health? Do you exercise? Do you cut down on your diet? Do you continue to sleep with the radio on? You must take control first, then you can talk about the rest."

"Can I ask you directly about my books?"

"Yes and no. You know that to answer directly would be a shock to the psyche, either way. It is left to the discretion of Divine Spirit what to say. It has always been that way. But this I can say, you and Penny have earned the grace and dignity that you seek for your golden years. Please trust me, they are coming and you will have the golden years of your dreams."

"That's all I ask..."

8. Letting the Chips Fall

Wednesday, July 16, 2014

"Good morning, Padre. I did it again yesterday. I let my lack of good judgment take over and jeopardized an opportunity. I emailed the writer Paul Hendrickson (*Hemingway's Boat*)asking if he would be interested in reading my new book *The Lion that Swallowed Hemingway,* and then I asked if he thought it worthy to endorse it. That scared him off. I know it, and I feel like a bloody fool again. Will I never learn?"

"You acted on your feelings. That is your nature. Sometimes they are right on, and sometimes they are off; yesterday I don't think they were right on, but they weren't off either. That is the beauty of being you. You have a depth to you that others do not, and what you say has more than one meaning. He will see that when he checks out your website. He will see your sincerity, so don't fret over it any more than you have to. Just get on with your life."

"Such as it is. I don't know what's happening to us, Padre. Something is going on. Our world seems to be getting smaller and smaller. I'm talking about the world that Penny and I live in, not the world at large; why do I feel this way, and why do I feel that we are being isolated from the rest of the world?"

"The world is compromised. You and your loved one are not. That is why the world shrinks from you. It is only natural when one walks their own path. It will always be this way. But you are not alone. You will find your own friends, your own community. The light shines for you."

"What trite! I don't know what to say. This massaging does me no good. It only prolongs the agony. I'm reminded of Jung's confrontation with the unconscious. He fled from such massaging of his emotions."

"And well he should...."

Friday, July 17, 2014

"I had to stop writing yesterday, so I never connected with you the way I wanted to. I was out of sorts. I took a sleeping pill last night and feel a little more rested today. I still feel out of sorts, but not as bad as yesterday. I just want to know, has my ship cast adrift? Am I floating out there somewhere?"

"You are in between projects. That's the state of mind of not being here or there, and you feel out of sorts; but it is the gestation period. You will be tapped on the shoulder again by your Muse, and you will be engaged. For now, keep yourself engaged by force of will. Edit your Sum book. Get it ready for Penny to edit and get it out after your Golden Seed. It will keep you busy, and it will do your writing career a lot of good. I like The Sum of all Spiritual Paths."

"Padre, why all these reminders of my past?"

"You have accomplished what you set out to do, and so your mind is going back to your youth. You set out on a course to find your true self. You have, and now you are being pulled back to where you started your journey from."

"The thought crossed my mind yesterday as I was reading on the deck of writing a short book on something like 'I Believe,' or 'My Philosophy of Life,' or something to that effect; the point being, that I would like to write in one little book what I have arrived at in my understanding of life. I've done that with all my books, but I have a faint vision of one book saying it all."

"When the time is right, it will happen."

"Did I presume too much with that writer (Paul Hendrickson)?"

"Yes and no. He was both flattered and surprised. He's not used to such personal emails from strangers. He has checked out your website, and he doesn't know what to make of you. He's reflecting."

"Is there any chance of him endorsing me?"

"*That's in the air. He's very busy, but he is also a seeker in his own right; and he's curious about your philosophy of life. The book that got to him was your Why Bother? He's going to look into your writing.*"

"The book that I want to write that brings it all together in one perspective—the one path perspective, which is our own life—is the book that crossed my mind yesterday. Don't all paths merge in the self?"

"*The self is the path. This is your point.*"

"But the self has to realise it before it says it, doesn't it? Isn't this the point of the book? The self that presupposes itself is not a realized self; it is a self in potential. That's what the journey of the self is all about, isn't it?"

"*That's the mystery that you have brought to light. That's the heart of the big secret. You have transcended the being and non-being of the self and see the self in progress from the point of view of the transcendent self and this bothers your readers because they cannot conceive of a self that is both being and non-being but neither. This is the crux of the problem. Whatever you say speaks from this perspective, and it has an effect on everyone who reads you. But that's neither here nor there. The voice is one, wherever it speaks from. The mystery is always revealed. It is never hidden. It is all a question of consciousness. How aware are they who hear what you have to say?*"

"Is this why I read the same books over again?"

"*Precisely. A change in consciousness equals a change in perception. It is the way of life. Just live your life and let the chips fall where they may.*"

"But I do so wish that my love and I go gracefully into the night. I do so wish that we—well, I don't have to repeat myself."

"*No, you don't. And I don't have to repeat myself. The way has been cleared, the driveway will be paved. Your life will unfold with the grace and dignity that you so desire. Just live your life and let the chips fall. That's all I can say.*"

"Okay. Thanks."

9. Where, O Where?

Saturday, July 19, 2014

"Good morning, Padre. Where is this taking me? I know that every book I write will find its own way, and given that I always write for literary intent, I should know by now where my new journey with you is headed; but I don't. Can you tell me?"

"As you say, every book finds its own way; just give yourself the freedom to let go and let Spirit. This is how you write your spiritual musings."

"I just glanced through The Sum of All Spiritual Paths and am amazed by what came through. Will these books of mine ever see the light of day?"

"Your writing is an acquired taste, but once acquired it will nourish the reader's soul like few books do."

"How do I get the reader to acquire a taste for my writing?"

"It takes time. One breakthrough is all you need. I know you've heard it before, but just keep plugging along. Patience."

"I'm useless unless I feel engaged. I need a new project to work on. Have I lost my connection with my Muse?"

"The well is filling up. It has been drawn for your last two books—The Lion that Swallowed Hemingway, and The Golden Seed. Patience."

"Am I wasting my time here? Who wants to read this?"

"Time is never wasted when one seeks their undiscovered self. Life is a mystery that never reveals all of its secrets. Just enough to keep you engaged in the journey to wholeness; and that's what everyone wants, whether they are aware of it or not. It is the driving need, just as Jesus said in the book you were reading this morning."

"Fair enough. But I'd like to clarify, if I may. Our greatest need in life is to realize our own divinity; correct?"

"*Yes.*"

"And we do that through the process of our own individuation."

"*That's one way of expressing it. I would prefer the journey of the self.*"

"Why?"

"*The self is who you are, and the journey of the self is a journey of self-discovery.*"

"Yes, but that's the quandary; isn't it? My whole journey has been one of self-discovery; but to discover my true self I had to *become* my true self. That's why I wrote that we cannot presuppose a self that has not yet become itself; can we? Because that's what the Buddhists do. They presuppose a self that has not discovered itself, or become itself. That's putting the carriage in front of the horse, and to me that's spiritually obtuse."

"*You are correct, but so are the Buddhists. They want to short-circuit the journey without explaining why.*"

"Do they know why?"

"*No. If they did they wouldn't be stuck on the Mental Plane. Like Jung said, you cannot individuate on Everest.*"

"And yet they try."

"*Yes. That's what they need at this time in their journey of the self.*"

"Okay, I know; every path is valid. Every path serves its purpose. Is this a closed system, then? Do we just go round and round and round until we get so dizzy and tired that we want out?"

"*Yes. This is how it works. This is the big mystery. That's what happened to you, and me; that's why we had to break the cycle. We got tired!*"

"Did we really arrange on the other side to meet on this side the way we did? Did we really arrange to work on my novel *Healing with Padre Pio*?"

"*Yes. We're old souls, my friend. We go back a long way.*"

"And my parallel life? You told me that I have lived my same life over again three times. Is this a regular thing for souls?"

"Yes. But a soul has to reach a certain level of maturity before it can return to re-live the same life again. It requires a certain kind of integrity."

"What do you mean?"

"Let me put it this way: not every soul that lives the same life over again breaks away and achieves a different outcome. Most repeat the same life over again and suffer the sameness, which can be very depressing. These souls have given in to the circumstances which they wanted to break away from. You broke away, and look at what it cost you. If you did not have the integrity to break away—and by integrity I mean the strength of will, the courage to do what you felt you had to do—you would have lived your same life over again."

"What about this business of the multiverse? Does every choice we make open us up to a whole new universe?"

"No. That is a misunderstanding. If every choice we made opened up a whole new world there would be nothing but confusion. It doesn't work like that. But now is not the time to get into this. Let it be for now. All you need to know is that parallel worlds do exist. You are living in one right now because you broke away from the life you have already lived. You are in the same life, but you are living it in a different state of consciousness. This is why you feel apart from everyone. The world you broke away from is still living its life in that state of consciousness that you broke away from. This sounds confusing, but it's not. Consciousness is always one, but your viewpoint determines your reality. Your viewpoint has altered. You have transcended yourself."

"Where does that leave me, then?"

"Your duty now is to open the gateway with your writing to this new level of consciousness that you have realized with your own life. Your writing is a gateway, as was the life of other souls that transcended themselves. Mine, if you want another example. Socrates, Gurdjieff, Jung—every soul that finds the way to their true self and lives it becomes a gateway to higher consciousness. That's the mystery and joy of every path. They are all uniquely the same!"

"The mystery of the transcended function?"

"Yes. Resolving the opposites. That's what it's all about. You have made a wonderful breakthrough with your understanding of enantiodromia. Your Hemingway book is going to find its way. I promise!"

"What do you think of my idea for a You Tube video for my Hemingway book? Maybe two or three videos?"

"That's what it needs. You Tube will do wonders for that book, and all of your books. Do a You Tube for every one of your books. Go with it."

"Give me your best advice on how to do my videos, please."

"Never, ever present yourself as THE ANSWER. Always, always be true to your journey. Don't apologize for your journey. It will speak for itself, but NEVER make of it more than it is. NEVER assume that it speaks for the Whole. Your journey is yours, even though it speaks for the Whole. This is the trick to staying humble. The Whole is you, but you are not the Whole!"

"So I have to let the Whole speak through me, is that it?"

"Yes. But always as you, never as the Whole. In other words, be true to who and what you are. Never be the Whole, because the Whole is beyond you, me, and every soul. The Whole is beyond all. This is the paradox of the Way. We are forever becoming the Whole, but the Whole is always us."

"Is this the secret of the Buddhist path?"

"In a manner of speaking, yes; but the Buddhist have, as you say, put the carriage in front of the horse. They have the mistaken notion that they are the Whole, but the Whole can never be realized because the Whole is always becoming the Whole. 'I am that I am,' said God to Moses."

"I'd like to know if I can pull this off. I do have a sneaky little bit of me that still wants to grab the spotlight. Can I keep it in check?"

"Yes. Just keep in mind that you do not speak for the Whole but that the Whole speaks through you. It's a fine line to walk. It took me a lifetime to learn how to communicate with life. My time in the confessional taught me how to listen to the Whole as it

spoke through each penitent. In listening, I learned the secrets of the Way. You learned the Way in your own way, and I learned it in mine; but we both resonate with the Whole in our own way. Just don't let that little part of you get a chance to steal the spotlight."

"How?"

"You need a reminder. Get an object to remind you. Hold it in your hand. Make it, as Gurdjieff would say, a 'reminding factor.'"

"How about my little statue of St. Padre Pio?"

"That would work. Stand it up by your phone camera while you are doing the video. It will remind you to stay humble."

"Thank you. And you say this is the way to go?"

"The sooner the better."

"Wonderful. Until the next time..."

10. We Are Not Meant to Know

Monday, July 21, 2014

"Good morning, Padre. I have several concerns. One: I have come to the realization that we are not meant to know the secret way of life; and two: even if we are meant to know, people don't want to know. That's what life has forced upon me. And this leaves me in a quandary. Your thoughts?"

"The secret way of life is there for everyone to see, hear, and live by; it is, as Jesus said, not hidden. The kingdom of heaven is everywhere. That takes care of your first concern, because only those that are ready to wake up to the secret way of life will be called, and if they choose to live the secret way of life—or enter into the kingdom, if you will—will live the Way. Many are called, but few are chosen, said Jesus; so it's not like it's hidden from the world. And for your second concern; I agree, people don't want to know. With this knowledge comes the moral responsibility of living the secret way of life; and people sense this and flee from it. But again, life is a process; and every person is at the stage of the process that they have created for themselves. When they are ready, they too will hear the call and will be given the choice to live the secret way of life."

"From this perspective, it doesn't really matter how life unfolds. All of these world upheavals, none of it really matters. Life goes on; right?"

"That's the bleak side, but yes; life goes on regardless. The positive side is that life goes on for a reason. Things happen for a reason. Learn the reason, and you learn how the process works; and then you can choose. You did."

"The process is the way of life and the way of Spirit, in brief?"

"Essentially, yes. The way of life is the way of the world; and the way of Spirit is the secret way of life. The two ways are one,

but the secret way of life is not seen until one is ready to see it. Those that have eyes to see, said Jesus."

"And ears to hear?"

"Yes."

"That's what I like about my novel *The Golden Seed*; it brings the two ways—the way of the world and the way of Spirit—into one story."

"Yes; and you did it in such a magical way that it will leave an impression upon the reader. You must get this one out; and do a video!"

"Back to my concerns. I see the logic, but I still suffer the effects of my separateness. Will I ever meet that secret society of the Way, if you know what I mean? Those who have chosen to live the secret way of life?"

"You will. But don't fret. It doesn't matter if you do or not, and when you realize this you will have enormous peace of mind. You still suffer the need for acknowledgement in your writing. It is a slow train to paradise, if I may be allowed a little humor."

"You may. It looks like we won't be getting together this summer for our next book project. I was looking forward to it. Will it happen?"

"I said it would, and it will."

"What are the chances that one of my videos will go viral?"

"Again, that all depends. Do it and find out what happens."

"I think I'm trying to build up my self-confidence. I feel a certain despair, a kind of fear that's lurking in the background; the fear of losing my connection with my Muse, if you will."

"That can never happen. Your Muse is always with you. It's all a matter of commitment and engagement. Once the commitment is made, engagement is soon to follow. It is all one package."

"I guess it's the spark that excites the commitment that I fear losing. I don't seem to feel that certain flow through me anymore."

"As I said, you have drawn from your well with your last two books. Let the well fill up before you make any rash decisions."

"Commitment. Maybe I should get *The Sum of All Spiritual Paths* ready for Penny to edit and format and publish?"
"I would welcome that."
"Okay. Thank you, Padre."
"You're welcome."

11. An Inspired Thought

Thursday, July 24, 2014

"Good morning, Padre. I may have broken through my bout of creative aridity yesterday with my spiritual musing "The Many Faces of Depression," but I don't think I'm out of the woods yet. My connection with my Muse is still a little weak."

"Good morning, my friend. To the point: the more you write, the better your connection will be. You know the principle of DOING, so apply it. It doesn't matter what you write, as long as you write because doing brings results."

"We got our driveway paved on Monday, three days ago, and I started spreading the top soil that we had delivered to the side of our house before they paved the driveway, and our front yard is starting to look better; and after I sow the top soil that I am spreading alongside our new asphalt driveway with grass seeds our front yard will be finished. And then I have to deal with the dreaded thought of going up north to tend to our triplex. I don't want to go, but it looks like I have to, and I'm calling upon you for help."

"Yes, you will go and tend to your triplex. It will be okay, I promise you. Your imagination has a way of preying upon you. It will all go well. There is no need to fear. The way has been paved for you, if I may be allowed to pun."

"You sure may. So, has the symbol of the paving of our driveway begun to kick into "paving the road of our life" yet?"

"Yes. As you say, it is a powerful symbol. The outer is a manifestation of the inner, and once it happens on the outer it means that it's already realized on the inner—both literally and metaphorically."

"Why am I so full of fear?"

"Fear is the unrealized energy of your undiscovered self. The more you discover yourself, the less fear you will have. Write! That is your light that shines upon your way. Just write and let it be!"

"I learned something about Facebook yesterday. People need Facebook to share their grief and hardships. It's like going to the therapist and laying on the couch and telling him all your problems. People need that. I made a comment on one's hardship and I felt like I had violated his couch time with his therapist, and this bothered me for hours; so I went back on Facebook and deleted my comment, and I felt that I restored his privacy. It was a very strange experience for me. It gave me a deeper insight into why people use Facebook. They need their "Facebook therapist" to hear their problems, just as the sinners that confessed their sins to you needed you to hear them; am I right in my understanding?"

"More right than you realize. The world is hurting, and people need their confessor. As long as you act from this perspective, your attitude towards Facebook will change. People who are hurting don't need wit or putdowns; they need to be understood and accepted in all their troubles. You were right to undo your comment. It was a violation of his intimate time with his Facebook friends, which, as you say, are his 'Facebook therapist.'"

"I think there's a spiritual musing in this. I wonder if I have enough material to write a spiritual musing—"

"Just give it to your Muse and see what happens. The creative process is its own light, and once it has been sparked there's no telling where the light will shine. Just trust your Muse—"

"Alright. Just for the fun of it, I'm going to try. Until the next time..."

12. The Pearl of Great Price

Monday, July 28, 2014

"Good morning, Padre. I've started re-reading *Entering the Castle*, by Caroline Myss, her book on the mystic St. Teresa of Avilla, and this has inspired an idea that I would like to run by you. Caroline says in the interview at the back of the book that St. Teresa guided her in writing *Entering the Castle*, very much like you say you guide me, with nudges, thoughts, and ideas; and I would like to know if you would be interested in exploring ideas with me in these dialogues."

"The concept would be far-reaching. Yes, by all means. You have one concept that you would like to begin with?"

"Yes. Caroline says in her interview that 'the more the world spins out of control, the more your interior world must assume full control.' This is something that you would say. But I'm too much of a realist to expect any miracles, and I know that the world finds its own way. I see a quandary here: do I express my concern through my writing and let the chips fall where they may, or do I even bother and write stories instead?"

"Why not do both? Your talent has been cultivated in both genres, and it would be a waste not to exploit the gift you have been given. So, where would you like our dialogues to go?"

"In truth, I would like the essential Padre Pio and the essential Orest Stocco (the one who has transcended his voice and the voice of his spiritual community) to dialogue on life and the secret way of life that is everywhere to be seen. I would like our dialogue to be genuine and not a reflection of my own mind. I would like our dialogues to be revealing, enlightening, and as entertaining as we can make them. That's what I would like."

"Then abandon to the process and let Spirit have its way with us. We are the same insomuch that we understand the way; so, begin with whatever concerns you at the moment."

"I don't believe the world is going mad. I'm inclined to believe what Jesus said to Glenda Green, that the world is perfect as it is, and it is unfolding to the Divine Plan of God. What is your view?"

"From the big picture point of view, I agree with what Jesus said; the Divine Plan of God is perfect in all of its aspects, and the world is unfolding as it would according to its own choosing. But down in the trenches, the world looks like it is going mad—as the current war in the Mid-East would indicate. It's a very complex situation, and the only way to make sense of it is to go within. In this respect, Caroline Myss has it right, and it is wonderful that she and St. Teresa are working together to wake man up to the interior castle of their soul. You, on the other hand, have a different mission. Your purpose is to bring understanding to the secret way of life. This is your forte. Which is why we are working together. I resonate with your understanding of the way, and together we can help to explain the simple path to God through the journey of one's own life. By making people realize that their own life is the way to the divine, you will have accomplished your mission; and you do this with all of your writing."

"Give me your definition of the secret way of life, if you would?"

"The secret way of life is the life you are living, if you live it with honesty, integrity, loving kindness, etcetera; it is doing what you were born to do, but in the awareness that you were born to live your own life and not another's. This is the secret that people need to be made aware of. The truth lies in your own heart, not out there somewhere. It always comes back to your own heart."

"I guess we have all been conditioned to believe that the pearl of great price lies out there somewhere, but it doesn't; it's in our own heart. But the irony is that we all go out there to look for it, and when we can't find it we sit down in despair and cry, Woe is me."

"Something like that. The one pattern that I began to notice in all the penitents who came to me for confession was the desire to be free of a life they no longer loved, and my greatest pain was in telling them that that was the life that God wanted them to live. **The pearl of great price is our own life.** *And once one realizes this they will stop looking for it out there. That's the secret way to God, just coming to terms with your own life and not desiring to live another. The parameters of your life can be expanded, but never abandon who you are; because in being who you are you are being true to your own divine nature."*

"I see where you're going with this. We, our own individuality, is the pearl of great price; and realizing our own individuality is what the journey through life is all about. Okay; so the ball is in our court: how do we realize our own individuality? That's what we should explore."

"There are many paths to the pearl of great price, and it doesn't matter which path one takes as long as one is true to the path because all paths lead to the pearl of great price; it's in the living of the path that counts."

"My experience informs me that when one has exhausted one's path another path appears. This is how life works, so we need not fear of ever running out of road, as it were."

"Precisely. All roads merge into one; or, rather, the road is one with many different expressions. Having the courage to continue the journey is what the struggle of life is all about."

"Just to be clear, the pearl of great price comes from the Gospel of Mathew, 13: 45-46. *"Again, the kingdom of heaven is like unto a merchant, seeking goodly pearls: Who, when he had found one pearl of great price, went and sold all that he had, and bought it."* Jesus has compared the kingdom of heaven to the pearl of great price. He has already revealed the kingdom of heaven in other parables, but the parable of the pearl of great price speaks to the price that one must pay to find the **kingdom of heaven**, which you and I know to mean **the secret way of life**. And, as you say, our own life is the pearl of great price; which means that our own life is the way into the kingdom of heaven—or, to be perfectly clear, as we live our own life in the spirit of Christ's teaching (whosoever doeth these sayings of mine shall not taste death, or as Jesus reveals in the Parable of the Good Samaritan, with love and compassion) he will have the pearl of great price. The problem is that people have confounded the parables of Jesus to mean what they would like them to mean; but when one has found the pearl of great price—or, more accurately, when one has paid the great price for the pearl of great price—one understands what Jesus meant by kingdom of heaven. This is why you and I are having this dialogue, because we have both been bought with a price, to use one of your favorite saint's expressions—"

"You do make me laugh. Yes, St. Paul does say that; he too paid the great price for the pearl of great price. That's why he's so profound in his understanding of the secret way of life—or, the kingdom of heaven, if you will; because kingdom of heaven and the secret way of life are the same thing. And our own life being the pearl of great price, it follows logically that by learning how to live our own life we enter into the kingdom of heaven—or, to be more accurate, we are initiated into the mysteries of the kingdom of heaven."

"What do you have against St. Paul?"

"Resonance. It's all about individual frequency."

"So, you don't resonate with St. Paul?"

"Not while I was alive. Now we're great buddies, as the saying goes. Remember, just because one lives the same teaching doesn't mean one always agrees. That's the nature of the pearl of great price. No two pearls are the same. This is the mystery of the divine nature of man."

"I understand. Okay, Padre; we've begun our dialogue..."

13. Pardon My Funk

Thursday, July 31, 2014

"Good morning, Padre. Well, what do you have to say on this grand day of mine?"

"The day is yours and you should be proud of it. You have come a long way since that day you were born in Reggio Calabria. I too did not celebrate my birthdays. I thought of them as just another day."

"I think I'm slipping into depression. This is new to me. I don't like this feeling. You are a man of hope. What the hell is going on with me?"

"You fear not realizing all of your dreams. You fear not getting all of your books out. You fear for Penny's security. That's your biggest fear."

"Are my fears ill-founded?"

"Yes. Your mind wants to keep you trapped in fear."

"Why?"

"That is one of the functions of the mind plane. Its purpose is to keep soul trapped in the lower worlds. Fear is the mind's biggest trap."

"Well I'm tired. I could have sunk into a real funk yesterday, and I may still slip into a real funk. What can I do?"

"Work on a story. Get yourself into creative mode. That will connect you with your inner self and the life force. Once you connect, fear disappears."

"Why do I fear writing my stories?"

"That's the real question, isn't it? You will always find something else to write before you get to your stories. This is because your stories are the best that you can do, and there is power in your stories. The fear comes from outside of you to keep you from writing them. I hesitate to say this, but you have been

fighting negative forces most of your life; and I think it's time you got a little help. With your permission, I want to help you."

"You have my permission. What can you do?"

"What I always do when I am asked to help. I turn to God. God never lets me down in my requests, and I ask God for help in your writing. I will say special prayers for you because I think it's time that you were set free from the negative forces that have beset you for so long. You have earned the privilege."

"Is this all smoke and mirrors?"

"It is what it is, and the only thing you can do is wait and see. In the meantime, why don't you start working on your stories? Your story "Regression" is going to be written, and it will be one of your best; but first, finish your book of stories that you have called Enantiodromia. This is a pivotal book for you. It will open literary doors. Go on, do it! Work on them. Read them, and start a new one and work on it. You will have it done before you know it!"

"Well, I did call up my file. Can I ask you about my health? Is my heart more damaged than I think it is?"

"You must exercise it more. Walk or bike ride. You have to build up your heart muscle to pump more blood so you can have more energy. You must do at least thirty minutes of walking or bike riding each day. You will notice an improvement within a week. Just do it!"

"Pardon my funk, Padre."

"No need to apologize. I understand how you feel. Just live your life as if you are the accomplished writer that you are. You have nothing to be regretful for. You have achieved the outcome that you meant to achieve, and we are all proud of you; and soon the world will be proud of you. I promise!"

"Thank you. Until next time...."

14. Life Is a Journey of the Self

Monday, August 4, 2014

"Good morning, Padre. So, when all is said and done life really is a journey of the self, as you say; and the rest is all superfluous. No; that's not the right word, but you know what I mean. But I hate to tell you, the more cognizant I become of this principle—that life is a journey of the self—the less comfortable I feel; because in this realization there is a feeling of not caring—like it doesn't really matter what I do, because what I do doesn't impact anyone but me, and that places an awful lot of responsibility upon my shoulders. Is that why I feel so lacking in initiative now? Because I am becoming acutely conscious that life is only a journey of the self that bears no relevance to the rest of the world?"

"The irony is that the more cognizant you become of your life being a journey of the self, the more impact you will have upon the world; because in this realization you will awaken others to the responsibility of the individual journey to wholeness and singleness of self—if I may borrow a phrase that you like to use."

"You may. But you know of course that I borrowed this phrase 'wholeness and singleness of self' from Carl Jung. In any event, what am I onto here? It seems that in the realization of our life being a journey of the self there is a loneliness that comes with it that is difficult to bear. You spent a lot of time alone in your prayers and in contemplation. You must have become acutely conscious of your lonely journey of the self. How did you deal with your loneliness?"

"I was definitely alone in my prayers and in contemplation. Much more alone than anyone can realize because of my stigmata. It was a very difficult journey for me, and I cannot begin to tell you the suffering that I endured; and I would not have

survived had I not sacrificed myself to Jesus. All of my pain was my glory, and my glory was my salvation; but only because I sacrificed my pain for the salvation of the world, just as our Lord Jesus did with his life."

"I'm curious to hear more. I know that this exercise, which I have called 'active imagination,' taken again from Jung's phraseology, may be just an exercise in creative thinking; but it doesn't matter to me where it comes from, as long as it makes sense and answers my deepest concerns. After all, Spirit is one; is it not?"

"It is. But the mind does have a way of interfering in the communication of one's truth. I am what I am, and in time you will decide if this exercise is active imagination or direct communication with me on the other side. For now, just go with it. It does you good to keep engaged with your creative spirit."

"I used to have so many little "tricks" to keep engaged with my creative spirit, but time has worn me down. Can I ever get it back?"

"Not entirely. Your body cannot respond to life like it could when you were young, and you used your body to engage your creative spirit through the act of physical doing. Physical doing was your entry point into the great currents of creative energy; but now you must employ other methods."

"I know. I could be doing so much more, but I am burdened with a thought that won't go away. A thought of my own making, but big enough now to immobilize my creative spirit, and I have to make enormous efforts to get engaged. Writing stories helps. I got into my book of short stories yesterday, my book called *Enantiodromia and Other Stories*; and I have to say that it felt good once I got over the hurdle of my immobilized self."

"And the more you do it, the less immobilized you will be; so there's your answer, which you've known all along. But just in case you need reminding, let me say it out loud: THE MORE YOU DO, THE MORE FREE YOU WILL BE!"

"Free from my immobilizing self?"

"Yes. Free to do what you love to do."

"I sense that you want to get back to the journey of the self. What is it you want to reveal to me? I sense you have something to say."

"As you know what Jesus said in Glenda Green's book, 'there is only the self and God,' you must appreciate the depths of that truth; and the only way to appreciate the depths of that truth is to engage yourself in this journey of the self, which should be the theme of our dialogues."

"Okay. I'm game. So, let's start with your journey of the self. How would you define or describe your journey of the self?"

"Mine was a journey of suffering. La via di sofferensa, as the way of the cross is called; but it was my personal cross. Everyone has a personal cross, though the phrase does not apply outside the Christian context, but the reality is the same. It is the journey of one's own karmic resolution, if that makes more sense to the non-Christian. I devoted my life to Jesus, serving his mission upon the earth; and I was blessed with the holy wounds of Christ so I could suffer my way to freedom. But I learned to sacrifice my suffering or I would not have lasted as I did. I would have gone out of my mind, and sometimes I thought I had; but I managed to hold onto my sanity and saw my way to the end. But mine was an extreme life, and it was my choice to live that way; and so is everyone's life born of the choice they have made on the other side. We make decisions on the other side as to what kind of life we are going to live, so on a deep level we are not unaware of our journey of the self because we have decided on a spiritual level to live the life we have chosen. You have chosen to live your same life over again to achieve a different outcome, and you have succeeded brilliantly; and now you have to deal with the effects of the outcome that you have achieved. It is a different reality that you live in, and you have trouble adjusting to the world; but the world does not really matter insomuch that life is a journey of the self. So do your best in what you do and let the chips fall where they may."

"I can appreciate that, but I'd like you to explain to me what you meant when you told me that I had transcended my own voice and the voice of my community. I presume you meant my spiritual community."

"Yes. Your' voice was not your own insomuch that you had not coalesced yourself into the wholeness and singleness of self that you were striving for; but your experience with me enhanced your journey of the self and you centered yourself in yourself and spoke from that place that was all of you. This is that special place in you where the knowledge and experience of all your lives is distilled, if one may use that word, into a single force; and that single force is the energy of your own individuated consciousness. This is what the journey of the self is all about—to center one in one's own individuation nature. And as to transcending the voice of your spiritual community, in the realization of your own voice you no longer spoke from the perspective of your community but from the perspective of your own individuated being. You were doing that anyway, which is why you were so much at odds with the voice of your community; but once you transcended your voice and spoke from the singleness and wholeness of self that you were, you no longer reflected the path of your community but your own individual path, which was the wisdom of your own journey. All paths are for the purpose of aiding soul on the journey of the self, and you transcended the path that was aiding you. That is why you feel as you do today. You are becoming more used to the reality of your own path, and your voice is coming through very nicely; that's why you had to wait to complete The Golden Seed. You had to be centered in your wholeness to bring this book to closure; and now you can write your stories with your own voice. That is why I encourage you to get back into your creative writing. Writing stories is your journey of the self, because in writing your stories you give complete expression to your voice; which means that in your creative writing you are most yourself."

"I hit a key that caused my text to magnify to 200% from 100%. Did you cause that for me to notice?"

"Not I; Spirit in me, if you will. Yes, life does have its magic moments. The point is that your voice is yours and not a mixed bag. And yes, you are correct to think that a writer who finds his voice early, or is born with his own voice, is way ahead of the game. This is what talent is all about. It's being who you are, the realized self of the long interminable journey of the self."

"I'm not quite there yet, but I'm beginning to see that this journey of the self is independent of the journey of the world; or, to be more precise, it's a journey within the context of the world but independent of the world. Am I getting closer to the truth with this insight?"

"The journey of the self cannot be realized outside the world, so it is interwoven with the world; but it is independent of the world insomuch that it is your personal journey and no-one else's."

"I'm having trouble grasping that. Does the world matter or not? What does it matter to me, for example, if the Israelis kill Palestinians and if Palestinians kill Israelis? It's their war, their madness; what does that matter to me in my journey of the self?"

"It matters insomuch that your journey affects the journey of the world. As you achieve wholeness and singleness of self, so does the world. Every drop of water adds to the ocean. You matter. We all matter. But all the same, it is an individual journey as you say; and the madness of their war is not your immediate concern. Your life is here, and the more responsible you are in your journey of the self the more you contribute to the sanity of the world. It is all one big puzzle, and each soul is a piece of the puzzle. But don't try to make sense of it. That is too big for one soul to appreciate. I could never make sense of it all, and I prayed to God for guidance in my journey. How often I suffered the despair of not knowing, and in the end I had to surrender to the simple reality that I was a lowly monk in a monastery and it wasn't my place to know the mysteries of the universe; and my life became easier in not knowing."

"But I have an imperative to know. That seems to be my nature. I want to know why. I want to know the mysteries. Or do I? The truth is that I am tired of seeking and reading and wanting to know. It has fatigued me. I can hear you laughing—"

"Yes. I am laughing. That is what happened to me. I too wanted to know so desperately that I fatigued myself. And then I surrendered."

"And the mysteries came to you in their resolution, no doubt?"

"Yes, of course; that's how it seems to work. That's why I keep advising you to write your stories and let the mysteries come to you in their resolution."

"Tell me again please why it's so difficult for me to get into my stories. What is this resistance?"

"Apprehension. You fear to enter where you might be forced to deal with your own unresolved self. This is every writer's fear. Why do you think writers suffer from writer's block? They fear going where their creative spirit wants them to go because when they go there they will have to deal with aspects of their nature that they have to become aware of to continue their journey of the self. Every novel (story) as you have come to realize is a thought that the creative spirit gives birth to, and this thought is the sum of the novel's process—or, if you will, the truth of the novel's process. And this truth is the resolved consciousness of the unresolved self that the writer fears to confront. That's why writers can suffer such darkness and despair while writing. Creative writing is a miraculous way to resolve the unresolved self. It is a direct path to one's true self, and the more you write your stories the more complete you will be because you will grow in your wholeness and singleness of self with each story you write. This is why you fear writing your stories, because they will take you to places you don't want to go—those darker corners of your soul, if you will. As I said in one of our healing sessions, life is also a journey of discovery—and peace."

"On this note, thank you for this morning's dialogue."

"You're welcome. Until the next time...."

15. The Process

Thursday, August 7, 2014

"I just read an interview by Goodreads with Paulo Coelho on his new novel *Adultery* and I'm in a kind of funk because I'm envious of his outrageous success as a writer; not that I don't think it's deserved, but that I feel he's a magician who has mastered the dark arts of marketing, and for some reason this annoys me—probably because I'm afraid to go there myself. I just thought I'd share this with you this morning just to start our dialogue. Oh, where are my manners? Good morning, Padre."

"And a good morning to you, my friend. Yes, I can understand why you feel as you do. Paulo Coelho is a world-wide phenomenon, and you are not off the mark in your feeling that he has mastered the art of marketing. Whether it is a dark art or not is left open, and we won't go there; but your gut tells you something that you should keep in mind. After all, he did study magic."

"I'm at loose ends. I've gotten into my stories and worked for the past few days editing and tightening up the stories that I wrote (this is for my book of stories *Enantiodromia*), and I am getting the pull; meaning, I do feel that I am engaging with the spirit of this book, and I want to go with it. But I have to ask you something: is the reality of these stories too stark?"

"Because they come from personal experience, they are very stark in the way you let the stories reveal their truth; but that's what is needed in the world today. There is not enough stark truth. There is too much spin."

"Where is all of this going?"

"I feel your discomfort. You are at loose ends. Engage in your stories and let Divine Spirit center you, because in writing you find your own center. That's why it's important to stay engaged in your process. The self is the journey, and as long as you stay engaged in

your process you are centered in the self—the personal self and the Self. You writing is your process. Remember that!"

"Will I ever raise myself above my worry belt?"

"In good time. You are caught in the throes of unresolved emotions. Once you complete a few of your responsibilities, you will be free of these emotions and more in your own space, as the phrase goes. Take one duty every day, only one and do it; one responsibility, and just do it. If you do two, fine; if three, better still. But train yourself to do one responsibility every day, and by responsibility I mean what comes to you that you feel you should do. Trust the process."

"Okay, I'm getting a feeling here that you want me to explore this concept that you have called "the process." I'm going to title this discourse "The Process," and we can take it from here. Let me give you my feeling about this concept, and then you can fill in the details. By process, I take you mean one's own way, or one's own individuation process; correct?"

"Essentially, yes. Every person is their own process. Every person individuates the self accordingly; meaning, according to their relationship with life, and no two people have the same relationship with life. The trick is to engage with the self, which can only be done with serious commitment to the object of one's desire—whatever that may be. In your case, it's writing. The more you write, the more you engage the self in the process of individuation; and the self becomes the Self. It's all one path. This is why I said to you that life is a journey of the self. Jesus said there is only the self and God. He could have said there is only the self and the Self. Both are correct."

"I get the impression that the concept of the self being the sum of all spiritual paths is what you mean by 'the process'?"

"Yes. But as I said, one must engage oneself in realizing the object of one's desire; because in the engagement the process begins. There is no process without engagement. Which is all about DOING."

"Tell me, is this where all paths—spiritual and secular—are heading? Does it come down to 'the process'?"

"*Generally speaking, yes; but that is much too elusive and abstract. The specific reality is that 'the process' is one's personal relationship with life and the cosmos. One's relationship determines one's process.*"

"You mean one's growth?"

"*In effect, yes. One grows accordingly. The more engaged one is in one's process, the more one grows in the self; and this leads to greater and greater horizons of spiritual growth—meaning, one gets closer to the Self.*"

"Alright, let's be clear. One's process is one's relationship with life; and the more engaged one is in one's desires, the more effective one is in one's process. Meaning, one precipitates one's growth as one throttles up the process of one's life, if I may express it this way?"

"*You may; and yes, the more engaged one is, the more active one's process will be. This is a simple concept that sums up all paths. This is the central idea of what you have come to realize about the essential nature of all spiritual paths and why you feel that life has played tricks on you all of your life. Life certainly plays tricks on everybody, and, as you say, plays people for fools; but that's the nature of the game of life. And I use the word 'game' deliberately. Everyone is after something in life, and how one gets it constitutes the 'game of life.' Learn how life plays the game and you will have the advantage. You have learned how life plays the 'salvation game,' and you got angry for being played for a fool because you awakened to the Way that is implicit to all ways, which is 'the process,' and now you are free to stand back and watch the world as it tries to figure it all out. It is an enantiodromiac phantasmagoria.*"

"I couldn't agree more! So, what do I do about my petty envy of Paulo Coelho's enormous success?"

"*It's not petty by any means. It's deep-rooted and serious. Use it. Let it drive your own process. Envy can be a powerful force, both for good and evil. Use it for your good. Don't fight it. Let it stoke the fires of your process.*"

"I feel that we're going to be talking more about the process; that this is the way of all paths, and the point of it all is to engage in one's own life instead of living life vicariously as seems to be the fashion these days."

"It's always been this way. People are always wanting to live another person's life. But once one engages in one's own life one will find that there is nothing more satisfying. Your life is your process, and learning how to engage in your own life makes your process your path, your way, your truth."

"Ergo, writing my stories!"

"Yes. Your writing is your process, your life, your way, your truth; and the more you engage in your writing, the more fulfilled you will be."

"Thank you. Until the next time..."

16. A Little More Moaning

Saturday, August 9, 2014

"Good morning, Padre. I don't know what to say or where to begin. I've just listened to a Dr. Joseph Martin talking about Paramahansa Yogananda's book *The Second Coming of Christ*, and I went to Amazon and looked it up; and, to be honest, I'm at a loss for words. How come I wasn't made aware of this book when I was working on *Healing with Padre Pio?*"

"It wasn't meant for you to know about this book. You had enough on your plate with what you had to read for your own book. Beside, that would have been a distraction from your path. Your path was to get to your own process, which is creative writing. Through creative writing you realize your spiritual destiny in this lifetime. You have come a long way in this, your second lifetime as Orest Stocco. You have been a wonderful surprise to us on this side."

"In what way?"

"You have connected dots that few people have connected. In your freedom to let your creative unconscious guide your writing, you have managed to see into the universal truths of the process as few souls do. This is why you must concentrate your energies on creative writing."

"What about this person that I was just listening to on You Tube?"

"He is on his own journey, and it is a course that would only detract from your own process. Entertaining, but not necessary for your journey."

"Does Jung really talk to him?"

"As you talk with me."

"Active imagination?"

"You could call it that. In his case, he is much more involved and much more caught up in his process. I cannot say more."

"What do you mean, 'As you talk with me'?"

"Your relationship with me is what it is. It has yet to find its center. In time, it will all fall into place."

"It is so easy to be pulled away from my process, isn't it?"

"Much more easily than you realize. The way is very narrow, and few stick to it. Creative writing is a very difficult path. Stick to it and you will be rewarded as you never dreamed."

"I'm not falling for that. What happens will happen. I don't want to be pulled into false expectations. I've been down that road!"

"Good. Then don't entertain the thought. Just let your heart be your guide and not your ego's desires."

"How do I distinguish the two?"

"The heart never lies, but the ego is all lies. It isn't what you are in your process. As you get engaged in your process you are your higher Self, and that's your heart speaking."

"I'm at a loss. Please, what to do?"

"Get some rest. It will come to you in your sleep tonight. Be of good cheer, the night will bring you hope."

"I hope so. Thank you."

"You're welcome."

17. Ontological Doubt

Sunday, August 10, 2014

"Good morning, Padre. May I impose upon you again?"

"You may."

"The night didn't bring me hope, and I'm no less anxious than I was before I went to bed; but I don't want to dwell on that. I want to know if my anxious feeling is brought about by my short stories. They're very personal."

"No doubt there will be some anxiety because they are so personal, but that's the nature of creative writing; at least, the best of creative writing. Literature is made up of stories from real life. This is the light that they carry, and the reason they are read by generations. You stories delve into the mysteries of human nature, and you have no need to feel anxious. They serve a higher purpose."

"Am I falling apart at the seams? I feel myself thinning in a way that scares me. I don't feel that connection with my creative self that always kept me centered in myself. What's happening to me?"

"What happens to every writer when they are in between books? As I have said, engage yourself in your stories and let the process center you."

"I know that I am most myself when I am most engaged in my process (working on a new book, that is), but I don't feel the calling that I would like to hear to engage myself in my book of stories; is that because I am still afraid to write the stories that I know I should be writing?"

"Yes. And because this kind of writing is very demanding. It calls upon your memories, and you don't want to go back there. Not creatively, that is. You have written about your life in other ways, but now you must confront the reality of your emotional

life; that deep, private self that you fear confronting. Don't fight it. Do it one sentence at a time. One true sentence at a time!"

"That's what Hemingway did."

"Yes. And that's what made him such a successful writer."

"Pardon me, Padre; but I'm going to take a break. I think I'm going to do some reading to see if I can firm up my connection with my inner self. Do you mind?"

"Not at all. Do your firming up and we can take it from there..."

"I'm back. Read for a while, and then had coffee with Penny and we talked about the book she is reading, *The Inspired Heart,* by Jerry Wennstrom; but she has a completely different take on this artist's journey than I have, and the more we talked about her impressions of the man and his commitment to his own process (he burnt his art and gave away his possessions and surrendered to the Universe to take care of him; he did this for fifteen years!), the more I saw her point of view; and it helped explain why she doesn't like the book. But being who she is, she will finish reading it. She started it and she has to finish it. That's how she is. Like the Hemingway novel *Across the River and Into the Trees.* She hated that book. 'It's the worst book I ever read,' she said; but she forced herself to finish reading it, and she's forcing herself to finish *The Inspired Heart.* But I loved the book, and we had to talk about our different take on it. And this inspired the title of this letter, and perhaps our dialogue— 'Ontological Doubt.' Would you like to explore this concept with me?"

"I'd love to. Ontological doubt is the essential cause of man's anxiety. It is the root cause of man's depression. Because man is so insecure in his own being, he suffers the agony of not being who he is. This is the life struggle. This is where the journey of the self begins—with ontological doubt".

"I feel myself engaging in the idea. Is this why I feel at loose ends, because I don't have a good idea to bite into?"

"You live by ideas. Ideas are your process. Yes; when you have an idea to explore, you activate your process and engage with the Source."

"By Source, you mean Divine Spirit?"

"The Source goes beyond Divine Spirit. Divine Spirit speaks for the Source, it is not the Source as such. The Source is God, for lack of a better word."

"This is getting deep, Padre. But I'm beginning to appreciate your term for the journey of the self, which you call the process. The process is one, but it is individual; and engaging in one's own life engages the process; is that the way it works? We are the Way, as it were; but to realize that we are the Way, we have to live our own life—or, live our own process as it were?"

"Yes. This of course renders all paths equal, because each person's process is as valid as any other's. But engaging one's process is what the struggle is all about, and it all begins with ontological doubt."

"This philosophical phrase came to me because of an article that I read in the April 15, 2013 issue of *The New Yorker* magazine: 'The Last Book, *Why James Salter isn't famous.*' The novelist James Salter said something that made a whole lot of sense to me, because it summed up how I feel: 'As a writer, you aren't anybody until you become somebody.' This inspired the concept of 'ontological doubt,' which I'd like to explore with you first before I decide to work it out in a spiritual musing. So let me explain why I feel as I do. I have written a number of books now (I think fifteen are published), but because all but one are self-published, and the other is published by a publisher that is not considered to be a mainstream publisher but is struggling vainly to become one, I just don't have the ontological security of being a published writer because my books are not yet acknowledged by the marketplace; they have to be out there and read by more readers than I am getting to confirm my sense of ontological security—meaning, my sense of being a writer. That's why I'm suffering the pains of ontological doubt. Just as Salter said, I am a writer, but I'm nobody until I become somebody. That's a fair description of my situation, don't you think?"

"Everybody wants to be acknowledged for who they are, and being a writer without the acknowledgement creates the anxiety of not being a somebody; meaning, the writer you are but aren't acknowledged for being. This is everyone's situation. Everyone wants to be acknowledged for who they are, even the criminal and the sinner. They all suffer the same doubt of being that the unacknowledged writer suffers. This speaks to the degree of one's spiritual sense of self. The more one is centered in one's spiritual self, the less ontological doubt they will experience; so the ontological doubt that you are experiencing speaks to your disengagement with your process. Because the more engaged you are with your process, the more spiritually centered you will be. Ontological doubt cannot be removed by pharmaceuticals or philosophy or psychology or religion even; it can only be removed according to one's commitment to one's process. This simply means that the more you engage in the living of your life, the more you will be engaged in the process and be centered in who you are; because you are most yourself when you and process become one. This is why the artist Jerry Wennstrom gave up on his art; because his process had taken him as far as it could, and he had to re-engage with his process in an entirely new way which would connect him with his spiritual self on a deeper level. His ontological doubt was enormous, as you should well know from your own journey through the dark night of your own soul; but he found his way through his dark night, as you did. And now he can speak freely about his process because he has risen above himself and speaks from a new level. It could be said that he transcended his own voice and the voice of his artistic community, just as you transcended your voice and the voice of your spiritual community. You both have that in common."

"But Penny made a point that scares me. She relegated Jerry's journey to that of the ordinary man and woman. Life is the way for her, and she's always had that deep sense about life being the Way; that's why she's not as moved by *The Inspired Heart*. Jerry's journey does nothing for her. She said that he comes across as some kind of saint, and that bothers her."

"I couldn't agree more. I came across as some kind of saint also in my lifetime, and nothing could be further from the truth. I was on my own journey, and my process was individual to me alone; but when I passed through the dark night of my own soul I also transcended my voice and the voice of my own monastic order and the voice of my religion. Then I spoke from a level of understanding that spoke for the process of every soul."

"And that's why we had such resonance. I loved talking with you, Padre. Even today some of the things you said in my spiritual healing sessions take on deeper meaning, and it's gratifying to know that you were real and not a figment of the medium's imagination."

"And I appreciated your acknowledgement. It made for a much wider scope in our communication. Belief opens doors, and you opened a wide door with your belief in me."

"But why is *Healing with Padre Pio* not taking off?"

"Give it time. It will find its place when the need for it arises. The need is soon approaching peak point, and then the tide will turn."

"I'm thinking of banking on *The Golden Seed*. I'm thinking of sending out copies to various people and publishers. I'm thinking—"

"By all means. You have to get it out there. It won't get out there on its own. Give it your best shot and let SYNCHRONCITY do the rest. Trust in the merciful law of synchronicity to work for you. It will!"

"I think I know where you're going with this. Are you saying that *The Golden Seed* is ready to find its place in the marketplace? That this novel is ready to fill the gap that's waiting to be filled, hence 'synchronicity'?"

"Yes; that's exactly what I'm saying. Synchronicity cannot work in a vacuum. There has to be a need for the law to kick in; and when that need is great enough it will attract something to satisfy that need. Your novel will satisfy a growing need for

answers that aren't coming from other sources. This is what causes success in life—the object satisfying the need; whatever the object may be—a person, a book, a movie, or whatever."

"Hold on a minute. I'm getting something more than I expected here, because this makes SYNCHRONCITY to be more than I realized. Is this getting closer to what you called 'the inner workings of the universe'?"

"In effect, yes. Synchronicity is a law of the universe. It is activated by need. When the need is strong enough, the universe has to respond to satisfy it. This is the inner workings of the universe, the drive shaft of life"

"So synchronicity is a law of the universe, then?"

"Yes. It is the law of need. When the need is strong enough, synchronicity must respond to satisfy that need. Apply this to any experience of synchronicity and you will see that it meets the criteria."

"So, does this mean that the need for my writing is not great enough yet to kick in the law of synchronicity?"

"Now you are beginning to understand. But the need is growing in direct proportion to the world's unfolding. The world is unfolding fast, and the need for your writing has almost reached that point where the law of synchronicity has to kick in. It's not quite there yet, but very close. Just keep on writing, and keep posting your spiritual musings. They activate the need, and the need activates the law of synchronicity. Which means that you can precipitate the process of your own literary career by letting your writing speak for you. Your writing wakes people up to their spiritual need, and the more aware people are of their spiritual need, the more you will attract the merciful law to satisfy that need; which means your books will gravitate to where they can be placed to best satisfy the spiritual need of your reader. Address the common man with the common problems and don't be afraid to take on the ordinary issues of the day, because in the ordinary issues of the day can be found man's greatest ontological doubt. It is everyday life that wears people down. Just read your posts on Facebook to confirm that fact. People are afraid and bored and *don't know where to turn; and so they post, and post, and post to overcome the doubt of their own existence—or, ontological doubt as you express it."*

"Okay. I get the picture. Thank you for our little chat this morning. It got me out of my state. I may go ahead and do a spiritual musing on ontological doubt. I know that sounds so philosophical, but I'm not going to write down to my readers. I never have, and I hope I will never have to."

"That's your process. Don't deny yourself what you have worked so hard to become. Your voice is yours alone, and no one else's."

"Okay. Until the next time, then..."

18. A Passing Feeling of Nostalgia

Tuesday, August 12, 2014

"Good morning, Padre. I've been reading some of our dialogues and I kind of like them for their spontaneity, if that's the right word. They speak for the moment, as it were; and that gives our dialogues a kind of freshness. I did write my spiritual musing yesterday. I called it 'Cricket in My Window.' Wasn't that an incredible coincidence?"

"Indeed it was. Good morning to you, and may the day bring you the blessing you deserve. Now, the coincidence of the cricket flying into your window. That was Divine Spirit speaking to confirm the thought of your musing, as you correctly interpreted; but it is much more. It is Divine Spirit establishing a better relationship with you to open you up to more wisdom. The language of synchronicity is the most direct way for Spirit to speak to man, and it can be cultivated. The way to do so is to engage in your process."

"Several things. This morning I leafed through a book that I devoured when I was caught up in my quest for my true self, *Teachings of Gurdjieff, The Journal of a Pupil*, by C. S. Nott, because I had a nostalgic feeling and wanted to re-experience the excitement of my quest; but the book didn't do anything for me. I read a few pages and put it back. I can't go back, can I?"

"There is no going back. The journey has been made, and now it is all about the process. You have found the answers you sought—which in itself is the most satisfying of any accomplishment one can have in life—and now it all remains in the DOING. This is where life begins in earnest. Up to this point, one must find the life that one must have to realize one's potential, and you have found it in creative writing—"

"Speaking of creative writing, yesterday I dug out a couple of manuscripts of short stories that I wrote a number of years ago and I'm rather excited by the challenge of reworking them into publishable form. I rather like them, regardless of how much I hate the author intrusion; but with a lot of editing and judicious cutting I'm sure I can make them work. What do you think?"

"I'm glad you dug them out. Those are the stories that speak from your own life, and those stories will garner you a literary reputation. Work them at your leisure. Do not dive into them. Work the stories you are writing now to get them out of the way, because in writing these stories you will bring that wisdom to your old stories. And yes, you will work them into little gems."

"What do you think of my idea of changing the name of my characters, to give them less of an autobiographical feel?"

"It will be a challenge, but a worthy one. This will extend the range of your literary voice, and it is necessary for your stories. It will give them a new dimension that will broaden the theme of each story. Go for it!"

"I intend to call one book of my old stories *Sparkles in the Mist, and Other Stories.* Did you like the title story?"

"It will be one of your best, and one of your most anthologized stories because of the emotional center of your story. It is real. This is what writing from the heart is all about. Yes, by all means; that's a great title!"

"Am I going to live long enough to get all these stories out? Because if I'm not, I'm—well, let's just say that as ready as I am to go, even though I don't want to just yet. I would so much love for Penny and me to have a few stress-free years in our life together. That would be so nice—"

"And you will. Don't worry about tomorrow. It will take care of itself. Just do what you have to do today, and leave the rest to God."

"Any advice on how to make my stories less autobiographical? By this I mean, how can I transform my alter ego (Oriano) and Cathy (Penny) into other people, because I feel that this is what I have to do to extend the range of my stories?"

"It will take some work, but essentially you have to relocate them to another geographical center. A new location distances them from your life, and then the characters will have more freedom to speak for themselves. As I said, it will take some work; but you can make Oriano a writer in another location, and Cathy a different person by little changes here and there. It will find its own way, I assure you; because once you give it over to your creative spirit, the stories will determine their own validity. This is how it works."

"I'm sure this is how most writers work. Hemingway's Nick Adams stories are autobiographical, but they don't read that way; that's what I want to do with my stories, but a little more distanced."

"Yes, many writers work that way. It all depends upon the writer's talent. Some writers have the gift of entering another world, the world of the great creative unconscious. These are the truly gifted writers. They let the archetypes speak for themselves, and their stories are created in that world to bring to light whatever the unconscious wishes to bring to light. There is no definite plan, as such; it is simply the process of the great creative unconscious."

"With no definite plan, as you say, does the great creative unconscious do this because this is what it does because of its nature? Or does it do this to expand the consciousness of man?"

"In effect, yes; but there is no definite plan. It would be a misdirection to think there is, because then we get into theology and God's purpose and all of that, which we will never understand. God is God, and God unfolds according to God's design; and try as we may, we will never understand. Ours is to be a part of the process and let the process unfold as God wills."

"Is this where you are right now, in the process?"

"In my own process, yes; and in my process I include everyone that I am assisting in their process. Mine is to expand the way for souls in search of God and wholeness and happiness. I love what I do."

"I quoted you on Facebook this morning, the bit that you said about ontological doubt being the source of man's anxiety; I quoted it on two Facebook posts by way of comment to the actor Robin William's suicide. I hope you don't mind me quoting our 'work-in-progress.'"

"It was an excellent choice. It was just the right note to offset the misunderstanding about depression. It is not a disease, as such; it is an emotional imbalance—I hesitate to use the word spiritual, so I will stick to the word emotional; and until one finds emotional balance one will always be subject to moods of depression. No, I don't mind you quoting me. It will be posted around the world now. Besides, this kind of thing boosts your confidence in our dialogues. It's all a part of your process."

"Am I correct in my understanding that the world is in transition from God-dependency to self-responsibility? I know it's a long road to hoe, but it has to start somewhere. Are we at the initial stages of this transition and the world in turmoil as the old demons hang onto their power over man's mind? Is this the reason for all the insurgencies around the world?"

"The world is definitely in transition, but it is much bigger than what you can see. It has to do with a shift in consciousness that is cosmic in origin. The world is only a small part of this shift in consciousness."

"Where does this leave us, then?"

"It all comes back to the self; the journey of the self; the journey of discovery; and the journey of peace. It doesn't matter what goes on in the world, it always always always comes back to the journey of the self. Once man realizes this he will stop running scared. You have no need to explore so much anymore. It has served its purpose to satisfy your need to know; but you know now that it's all about the journey of the self—so just engage yourself with you process and let the world unfold on its own. It will anyway."

"I get it, but executing the understanding is another matter. That's where I'm at—the execution stage. I'm reluctant to execute my process, for whatever reason. Can you tell me?"

"You have always been a procrastinator when it comes to exercising your will upon your inner life—resolving the deep-seated emotional conflicts. But when you do sit down to write, you do get engaged; and that's when you are at your most efficient and productive level of personal excellence. That's where you shine the most, like in your spiritual musings. They are a joy to read!"

"For you, maybe. What about the public?"

"The people who do read your spiritual musings are fascinated by your process. They can't figure out exactly what you mean by 'giving' it to your Muse. That disturbs and fascinates them; but they cannot deny the thoughts that come through in your process, and this shifts their paradigm."

"Actually, now that you mention it, this is a rather unique process; I've never come across anything like this before. It's like automatic writing, but it's entirely different because I'm in control of my engagement with my Muse—or, my creative unconscious to be more precise. In fact, my process of writing my spiritual musings has evolved into this dialogue with you, hasn't it?"

"Yes. This is the evolution of the technique of letting go and letting the creative unconscious speak; and it will evolve even further. Much further."

"I'm going to go over to my neighbor Tony's yard and pick some pole beans for dinner tonight. Remember the pole beans, Padre?"

"Very much. My mother loved pole beans, and we had them every season; they helped to sustain us. Mother used to dry them for the winter."

"I dreamt of my mother last night. I have to ask you something. My relationship with my mother on the inner planes (as I remember through my dreams that is) is not very satisfying. My mother is very distant from me, like we exist in two different worlds. Is this the case?"

"You hurt your mother very much by not coming to her bedside when she was dying. She will take a long time to forgive you. Your mother was a very proud woman. This is where you get your pride

from. She gave you much more than you will ever realize, because her spirit was indomitable. She did all she could to help you with what she had, but she feels in her heart that she failed you; and she holds herself responsible. Don't be too hard on her."

"I'd like not to be, but it's very hard to not hold my mother and my father accountable for much of our family dysfunction. It's an awful lot of stuff that they gave us to work out, and I'm not quite sure that was fair of them. They should have worked that stuff out themselves. Instead they gave it to their children to work out, and that's what most of my journey of the self was all about. I don't know if I'm right or wrong on this, but that's how I feel."

"If that's how you feel, than that's your truth and your reality. Your mother and father had their truth and their reality also."

"I'm reminded of what you said to me in one of my healing sessions for my book *Healing with Padre Pio*. You said that I needed that (stuff) to get to where I did; but does this condone the stuff my parents gave us? I don't think so, because there are many ways to get to here from there, aren't there?"

"Indeed there are, and that's what our dialogues are all about—to let your reader know that there is more than one way to get there; and by there I mean to wholeness of self and happiness and peace."

"So, my mother is keeping her distance from me in my dreams because I hurt her? What about how she hurt me? Is she aware of that? And what about how she was comforted (and quite possibly healed) when I sang the Love Song to God to her when she was hit with a touch of dementia?"

"Yes, you were the loving son; and she does thank you for that. But the hurt is deep, my friend; and it will take time for her to heal. You cut to the quick because you were so precious to her."

"Then why did she cut me out of the family loop?"

"The choice was forced upon her. She had to choose the side that supported her in her pride. You did not support her in her pride. You threatened her pride with your spiritual integrity. You threatened everyone in your family with your spiritual integrity;

but they are warming up to you now. They do check you out on your blog and they do peruse your books; but it is too much for them to take in, and they flee once their curiosity has been satisfied."

"That seems to be a common thing with people in my life. But hey, to each their own process; right?"

"Yes, to each their own process; and when the twain meet, they meet. But don't expect your family to embrace you. That won't happen in this lifetime. You have moved on too far for them to appreciate you for who you are. But they do respect you for your endeavors. You have surprised them all."

"Maybe I have, but I still would love to have that family feeling that families have; I do miss it. So, I'm off then to pick pole beans. Thank you for chatting with me today. Until the next time..."

19. You Make Me Smile

Thursday, August 14, 2014

"Good morning, Padre. It's five o'clock and I think I'm going to go downstairs and put on the coffee before we get into our dialogue. I don't know what I want to talk about yet, but I think it has to do with writing stories. If you will excuse me for a few minutes..."

"Good morning, my friend. Let's begin by saying that your perception of the story being a better carrier of the message is correct, because the image of the message is better conveyed by story than any other genre; so by all means, concentrate on your story writing because that's the most fulfilling kind of writing that you will ever do, despite how much you love writing your spiritual musings and having these creative dialogues with me."

"These creative dialogues are an exercise in active imagination, and as I've already indicated, I don't know just how real you are; though I suspect that there is a great deal of reality in our relationship because I won't allow myself to slip through the cracks into the fantasy world of my own mind."

"It is an exercise in active imagination; but what did Carl Jung do? He created the term 'active imagination,' but the entities that he met in the unconscious convinced him that they were real. Philemon could not have been a creation of Jung's imagination, as such; he revealed things to Jung that he never knew before. Trust the process. Let Spirit guide you."

"When Jung abandoned to the process of what was to become his 'confrontation with the unconscious,' he let go and felt the bottom drop out from under him; and he entered into a relationship with his unconscious that opened him up to the spirit of the deep. I'm afraid to let the bottom drop out from under me. I don't want to go there. When I was in France I got sucked into the fantasy world of my own mind, and I'm afraid of that happening to me again. So I cannot abandon to the process the way I wish I could. Does this mean that I don't trust you enough? That there's a part of me that suspects you're only a part of my own creative unconscious? I want this to be a real connection with you on the other side, but I have no way of knowing for certain unless you prove it to me with conviction. But I don't want to be one of those that has to feel the wounds on your hand to know that you actually did suffer the stigmata. I don't want to be that kind of person."

"Then don't be. We had a relationship for your book Healing with Padre Pio, and you believed in me then; just continue as if we were doing another book, only this time with no medium to convey my thoughts to you."

"Okay. Letting go, then...I'm getting closer to the date where Penny and I have to go up north, and the thought scares me. I don't know why I'm so afraid, but I have to see this thing through. And why am I dreaming of my hometown so often. I'm so tired of those dreams. Why do I have them?"

"You have a lot of memories there. You have lived that life twice, and you broke away. Your dreams are your memories of the life you lived there to the end, and you are only catching up on what you did. You want to compare your two lives, and your dreams are more memories than creative dream experiences; or, to be more accurate, they are a combination of both. But more memories than creative dream interpretations. And as to your trip up north, just let it happen. I will be with you every step of the way, and I will see to it that nothing bad happens to you or Penny. My love for you is great, and I would like to see your life completed to the fullest of its potential. No harm, no embarrassment, no humiliation, and no surprises. Just go with it and trust God."

"I want to cry. I want to open the floodgates and let it all out, but I cannot do that. I'm too uptight. I wish I could do it all over again! No, not really; but I do wish that I could have the experience of having done it right the first time, then I wouldn't have all these feelings of regret for not doing it right, which I have for so many things that I have done in my life. Is that why I came back to live my life over again—because my regret was too great?"

"Yes. Feelings of regret will compel one to repeat his life. You felt such deep regret for not realizing your goal of writing that you had to come back; but in your return you opened up the opportunity to look for the Way, and you became a seeker first and writer second. This was a double blessing. And your first life you lived to satisfy your material life but not your spiritual. That's why you died in that life full of regret. That's why you keep going back there in your dreams. You want to re-experience that life so you can feel good about the life you chose to live over again with your accomplishment of having found the Way and all the books that you have written. You did transcend yourself."

"I do want to thank you for my spiritual healing. That was the turning point of my life. I have to tell you that upon reflection Divine Spirit chose you to slay my vanity, because my vanity was so great that it took a Saint who had suffered as much as you did with the holy wounds of Jesus for fifty years to be humbled enough to slay my vanity; and I don't know if I can ever thank you enough for helping me shed myself of that shadow part of me. I don't think I will ever be able to convey what I mean when I say that my vanity was so great that it took a humility of greater depths to slay my vanity, and you were the Saint that Spirit chose for me. Can you explain what I'm trying to say?"

"Yes. The dragon needed a dragon slayer. I was called to be your dragon slayer because I have a history of slaying dragons. That was my life. I had to slay my own dragon before I could become a dragon slayer, just as you slayed your dragon by living the Way. We are the same. Only you don't want to give yourself the credit you deserve. But we are the same!"

"Padre, am I correct in my story perception when it comes to my spiritual community? I feel that I am being too honest. It's going to be tough on those that read my stories; but isn't that what my mentor would do—tell it the way it was? That's what creative story writing is all about—to tell it as it was and make it truer than it was. What do you think?"

"I think you are the writer that you are supposed to be in your stories. You have gone beyond what can be asked of you in telling it as it is, and your stories will do very much to help people see the truth about the spiritual life. It doesn't matter what path one is on, you are correct to point out that every path has a dark side; that's all you have done. Don't feel that you have done something wrong. You have written stories that point this out, and in images that will not be forgotten. Don't doubt yourself. Trust your creative instinct."

"Some people will be hurt by my stories."

"For a while, but they will see the truth of what you wrote and will change their attitude about you. This is the way of all writers."

"'There is nothing to writing,'" said my mentor Ernest Hemingway. 'All you do is sit down at a typewriter and bleed.' I guess that's why writing from the heart is so hard; it takes courage to tell it the way it was, doesn't it?"

"Yes. Courage and the desire to tell the truth. Writers are driven to tell the truth. This is their reason for writing. It is the spirit of truth-telling that drives the writer. They may not get it all right, but they get a lot of it right; and what they get right bothers a lot of people. But that's the way life unfolds. Life has to make things right, and writers are called to help make things right. You have been called to make right what you have experienced to not be right. You had to live it to experience it before you could write about it."

"Like my story 'The Sunworshipper' that I still want to write?"

"Yes, like that story. You will write it also. It will tell it the way it was, and it will be an eye-opener for your reader. It will be— correction, it is one of your best stories. As I said, just go with it. Trust God."

"You keep telling me to trust God. Have I so much doubt still?"

"Not so much doubt as fear. You have been hurt, and overcoming hurt takes a long time. Hurt breeds fear of

commitment. This is what you have to work on now. Trusting God is the best way to rid yourself of fear of commitment, because by trusting God you abandon to a Higher Power. You need the Higher Power to make your life easier. Doubt is a nasty thing to have. I had to fight the dragon Doubt most of my life. I know what you are experiencing, and I want you to know that your fear comes from the hurt that you have experienced; but you are on your way to being healed and your fear will disappear. I promise!"

"Thank you. Your words, whether they come from my creative unconscious or you on the other side, I don't care at this stage of the game; I'm grateful that you are so promising to me. It gives me courage."

"You're welcome."

"I'm going to work on my stories now. I think I have been sufficiently buoyed to get on with my day. I hope so, anyway."

"Dive into your stories and let the creative spirit carry you to where you are the most confident and efficient and fulfilled. Have a blessed day, my good friend. I am with you every step of the way".

"You make me smile. Until the next time."

20. The Weary Hour Coincidence

Saturday, August 16, 2014

"Good morning, Padre. I woke up this morning feeling like hell. I don't' sleep well, and last night was worse than ever; it took me a long time to fall asleep, but I finally did. I had the radio on all night, and I woke up now and then to shift my body from side to side. I know that my lack of sleep contributes to how I feel, but I can't seem to break the habit of sleeping with a radio. I need something to distract my mind. This habit started when I had a bad work experience many years ago with a contract that went sour on me on the Indian reserve near my hometown. I lost a lot of money on that job, and I became an insomniac; and I never recovered from that experience. But what I want to mention this morning is the odd coincidence of the short story that I read while I waited for the coffee to drip a fresh cup. The story is called 'The Weary Hour,' by Thomas Mann; and it's about the dread that comes to the writer in that 'weary hour' when he fears to write because of self-doubt—which was exactly how I felt when I got up this morning. So, what do you think of that coincidence? Is that Divine Spirit trying to cheer me up?"

"It goes to show you that you are never alone; that God is always watching over you. Yes, you can call it Divine Spirit; but why don't we cut to the chase and simply call it God, because it is God's will that you be happy in your journey back home to the Higher Worlds."

"And does the resolution of the story 'The Weary Hour' bear significance to my own writing, because the writer in this story does sit down and completes what he was writing?"

"Of course. It's all relevant. The story was meant for you to draw confidence and strength in your own ability, and it is foretelling."

"I've tightened and edited the first ten stories of my book *Enantiodromia and Other Stories,* and I have to comment on the stark realistic perspective of my narrator. Does he not have a disarming perspective? Won't these stories scare the crap out of the reader for their blatant honesty?"

"They definitely are honest, but I doubt that it will affect the reader that way. I'd be inclined to say that the reader will forego any opinion and take the stories for what they are: deep insights into human nature. Some of the stories, like 'In Her Red Shorts'will please a lot of readers, because it will show how the narrator was able to rise above his prejudice and accept her for who she was; and your story 'Needs and Creature Comforts' will speak to a lot of readers, especially women. These are some of your best stories, and you must finish this book. Write ten more, if you can; or enough to make a nice little book. It will go a long way to firming up your reputation as a literary writer."

"What did you think of my story 'Asshole'?"

"The title says it all. Readers will get a whole new understanding of what it means to be labelled one. I enjoyed it very much."

"Obviously, the narrator of Thomas Mann's short story 'The Weary Hour' was Thomas Mann himself. Last night Penny and I watched the movie based on his novel *Death in Venice,* starring Dirk Bogarde; and we enjoyed it very much because it gave us a lot to talk about. Thomas Mann was a true artist in the sense of being a spiritual explorer with his writing, and I know he was a terribly conflicted soul; but as he shows us with his stories, the impasses of his life are self-inflicted. In this sense, art is not enough to raise one above the drama of one's own enantiodromia; one has to live a life that is inherently self-transcending. That's what I discovered in my quest."

"I agree. I also discovered that through my penitents that came to me for confession. They taught me that without God's help they would never break free of their sinful habits. Yes, one does need help from an outside agency. You found it in the teachings that you studied, beginning with Gurdjieff's teaching; and you learned

to incorporate the principle of each teaching into your own path. That's how you transcended yourself."

"Padre, can you tell me how I come across on Facebook? I have a feeling that I am so far removed that my Facebook friends are afraid to comment on anything that I post. Why is that? Because I have transcended the voice of the person they knew and cannot relate to my transcendent voice?"

"Very much so. Your voice soars to the heights, and the heights give them vertigo. Do not fret. They admire you from a distance. And we should leave it at that, because to seek further explanation would only complicate things."

"I don't want to be fearful of what I write. I want to feel good and proud of what I write. But because my stories are so personal, I do feel a sense of trepidation. How can I rid myself of that feeling?"

"As you said, to tell it as it is you have to write fiction. This should be enough reason to rid yourself of trepidation. A story is a story is a story, and life is life is life; and when life meets story, the truth will win out. It always has, and it always will. It may take some time with some stories; but as history has shown all good stories will find their place in history. Yours will. I promise you!"

"And I need not fear any repercussions?"

"No. The story will speak for itself. People will get over it. There is no law that forbids you from writing about your own life. You take the facts of your life and write about them creatively. That's what fiction is all about. Don't give yourself a headache for something that's not going to happen. When one of your readers recognizes himself or herself, it will sting for a while; but they will grow from the experience. Life wins out in the end. It always does."

"What does that mean? Does it mean that the accounts will be settled? That score will be set straight? That reality will overcome illusion?"

"Yes. Life always wins out in the end. It may take a long time sometimes, but it will win out. Your stories may be too strong for the day, but life will acknowledge them over time. This is the way life works. What life cannot win today, it will win tomorrow; and

since there is no tomorrow in the grand scheme of things, life always wins today. So just write and don't worry about how your writing is going to affect the people you write about. Life is fair game for the writer. That's the nature of the game of art. How else can life win out if not for the artist telling it as it is? This is the point of the story 'The Weary Hour.' Thomas Mann is obligated by his art to listen to the sound of life when he holds the seashell of life to his ear. This was his calling, his duty, and his passion; but he dreaded the act of writing because it demanded so much of him. Which is the same feeling that you had this morning when you dreaded going to your stories. You feared going there because the sound of the seashell of your life is so vibrant with the naked truth of life; but don't be afraid of the truth. Life will win out. Just keep that in mind whenever you are working on a story: LIFE WILL WIN OUT. Just write your story and let your creative instinct be your guide. That's why God gave you the little boost this morning with the coincidence of Mann's story. God wants you to write your stories so your reader can see how life works from the perspective of one who has connected enough dots to create a satisfying picture of life. Don't hesitate in your writing; let the thoughts flow freely."

"I'm thankful for your guidance. It comforts me very much. If only I could act upon it; that would put the icing on the cake!"

"But isn't that what it's all about—breaking free of the habits that keep one from his calling? There's no shame in procrastinating when one understands how life works. It's supposed to work this way, because tension is the spice of life. Through tension you get the many textures of life, and this adds to the variety and many flavors, which only makes for better material when writing; not to mention the added incentive."

"I wish my Muse would tap me on the shoulder again. I feel that my calling to complete Enantiodromia and Other Stories is not strong enough to combust my fire enough to excite me; so what can I do about it?"

"Sometimes you have to work through the dull days. If this is how you feel about your book of stories, then trudge your way

through it until you complete it; and then your Muse will reward you with a new project. I promise you!"
"And trudge I must, then..."

21. The Treasure underneath All the Muck of Man's Ego

Sunday, August 17, 2014

"Good morning, Padre. I'm not in the right mood to start working on my story 'Lady Godiva and the Children,' so I'm going to chat for a while. I hope I'm not taking you away from something more important."

"Whatever I am doing, I will always make time for you. It's not that I am restricted to one task; I am free to multi-task, as the phrase goes. This is the joy of being one with Divine Spirit. And if I may, good morning to you too."

"This is a good point of entry, being one with Divine Spirit. This is what the journey of the self is all about, isn't it? Becoming one with Divine Spirit? I came to this conclusion a long time ago; that's why I've grown to see that there is no distinction between spiritual paths, because they all function to serve the purpose of making one become conscious of their oneness with Divine Spirit. And this is what made me angry with some teachings that think they are the only way to become one with Divine Spirit. Have I been going too far here?"

"Nobody likes to be played for a fool, and anger is sure to follow when one wakes up to the reality of his life; so you reacted in anger when you learned the truth about your spiritual path, that it was no more direct than any other because all paths to God are, as you say, equidistant. But it wasn't that so much as your enthusiasm for this teaching, which revealed itself in your emotional evocation of its principles which you later regretted doing because in retrospect they made you look like an overzealous believer. You got angry at yourself more than you did at the teaching. But that was your way, and this gave you the experience you needed to process your shadow personality. It's an

individual journey, and every soul has its own relationship with life. Don't fret over what you feel sorry for; just accept the fact that you did it, and move on. You have processed most of that energy, and the rest will be processed over time; but to dwell on your humiliations will only empower your shadow and take away the joy of your daily life. Be free to enjoy your day. Don't let worry drag you down."

"How did you overcome worry? Don't tell me. You prayed. You prayed the rosary to keep your mind off worry; right?"

"And I kept myself busy. When I was allowed to hear confessions, I spent all the time I could listening to my flock. They came to me to be close to God, and I did everything in my power to make them feel they were. But I did worry also. I was a constant worrier. Poor people are born to worry. It is built into their character. You come from a long line of worriers also. It is one of the defining traits of southern Italians. So you have a history of worrying that you have to fight against. But this too worked for you, because you had to fight to have your seed sprout in the light of hope and acceptance. It is nice to be given a good start in life, as many children have; but each soul's relationship with life is the result of their own doing, and where they find themselves in life is where they are meant to be. This is the only way to look at it with any degree of fairness; otherwise one will always curse the fates for not giving them more advantages in life. This was my constant struggle with my penitents. They always felt sorry for themselves until I told them that God wanted them to learn from their troubles, which I believed then and still believe today. Our troubles are our path to oneness with Divine Spirit, and learning how to embrace our troubles is what the spiritual life is all about. If only one could see the gold in the troubles one would not be so quick to curse them. The gold in one's troubles is the hidden treasure of one's life, and learning how to mine the gold of one's troubles is what I learned how to do in my life of suffering the holy wounds of Jesus, because I learned to let my suffering be my way to oneness with God. With every sting of pain I felt closer to Jesus, and in my daily suffering I inched my way closer to God."

80

"Could it be properly said that the suffering that you endured with the holy wounds of Jesus was symbolic of man's suffering in whatever circumstances of his life—man's suffering in general?"

"Yes. It was symbolic, but only too real. The symbol is only effective when it is lived. I lived the stigmata, and in the living the suffering of Jesus—which was his sacrifice for the world—became symbolic of man's suffering; hence, my connection with my penitents who came to me with their suffering. That was why I had so many people come to me for confession. They were suffering, and they came to me to help relieve them of their suffering; and I helped them to understand that there was spiritual joy in their suffering if they embraced it like Jesus embraced his suffering. That's the difference between suffering in the world and suffering for God. Embrace your suffering. Don't curse it. Find the joy in your suffering. This doesn't mean you should go out and look for more suffering; that would be foolish. But when suffering comes, embrace it. There is great joy in embracing your suffering, because as you embrace your suffering you embrace God's will. And God will reward you with the joy that comes from the resolution of your suffering. Suffering cannot last, because in this world nothing lasts forever. Everything must change, and so with suffering. Once the cause of one's suffering has been processed through the pain of suffering, then the suffering has to stop. Take a disease, for example. Once the disease has run its course the suffering has to stop. The disease could lead to one's death, but death puts a stop to the suffering caused by the disease. Everything has to come to an end in this world, and so does suffering. By embracing suffering one embraces the law that causes suffering, and when one embraces the law that causes suffering one embraces God; and God will reward you in your surrender, because in your surrender you let go and let God, as it were. This is how miracles happen. In one's surrender, God takes over the process. One's relationship with one's karma changes, because now God is in charge of one's process. Like your character Jordan Hansen in your novel The Golden Seed. He had to learn to surrender to the toss of the coin; and in his surrender he forfeited

his will to God, and God gave him the opportunity to change his life. This is the miracle of embracing one's suffering. It is in the surrender of one's will to God."

"Then what about the attitude that says things like this: 'I'm going to beat this cancer if it takes every ounce of energy that I have! I will fight this thing to the end! I'm not going to give up! I will beat this thing!'"

"It is very difficult to surrender to God, especially if one has difficulty believing in God, or if one's doubt of God is too strong. This is always a concern, and the fight to have one's will overcome one's karma is a losing proposition, because one's karma will always win out. It is the law of life. Isn't this what you learned when you wrote Healing with Padre Pio?"

"Now that you remind me, yes; and if I'm not mistaken, the divine law of synchronicity (God's love, if you will) brought me a cancer survivor to make my point—the Jungian analyst Marion Woodman. Her book *Bone, A Journal of Wisdom, Strength, and Healing* makes your point exactly about surrendering to the will of God. She sums up her healing from terminal cancer with this line taken from the Forward of her book: 'Fate is the death we owe to nature. Destiny is the life we owe to soul.' And by this I take her to mean that she surrendered to her fate (karma) so that she could live her spiritual destiny. I see your point, Padre. I had to surrender my vanity to free myself for my destiny; is that what you are trying to say? That by embracing our suffering we surrender our fate to life and engage our spiritual destiny?"

"Yes, that's a good way of putting it. Karma is a difficult concept to convey, and it involves much more than cause and effect; but for the purpose of this discussion, it is enough to say that in one's surrender to one's fate one embraces God's law. And when one embraces God's law, one allows the spiritual principle of life to work its magic; and the magic of Divine Spirit is compassion for every soul that seeks to be made whole. This is where trust comes into the picture. One must trust God. But I will give you a little tip. God is all compassion. There is not one part of God that is not compassion. So in one's surrender to God, one surrenders to

Compassion. *This is the miracle of one's surrender, because once God takes over one's process (suffering), one's relationship with God changes, because one is now embraced by Compassion. And Compassion activates all the factors in one's life that bring joy. I cannot tell you the miracles that I experienced when I felt compassion for my fellow man. By embracing the suffering of my fellow man, I entered into the holy world of Compassion. This is why I became known for my compassion. But little did the world know how much it meant to me to let God's love touch my fellow man every time I embraced my fellow man's suffering. Suffering is nature's way of correcting life, and it will always be with man; and the only way to deal with suffering in man's ignorance of the law of karma is to embrace it as Jesus did. This is why he died on the cross. He suffered to give man the symbolic gateway into the kingdom of heaven, because through the symbol of his crucifixion Jesus opened the gateway to the joy of man's connection with God. Christ's compassion for his fellow man allowed God into man's life, and once the love of God began to flow through the consciousness of society with every person who embraced Jesus as their savior, the law of resonance began to change the world. Jesus brought the highest vibration of Holy Spirit into the world with his death upon the cross, because Compassion is God's love. This is the topic of today's discussion, and I am happy that you opened this door. So embrace your suffering for the joy that it will give you. Do not curse your circumstances. Whatever suffering you may feel from your circumstances, that is only the fate of your life working itself out; and all you have to do is embrace it to activate your spiritual destiny, which is to become one with Divine Spirit. Any more questions?"*

"Not really. I feel like all the air has been let out of my balloon."

"You do make me laugh. I do so look forward to the day we can be with each other face to face. You are a stubborn, but precious person; and I would drop anything to help you in your journey."

"I'm stubborn in myself, aren't I? I refuse to do what I know I must do to continue my journey. There has to be a specific root source for my stubbornness. Is it a past life?"

"It is one of the residual effects of the vain life. You have come a long way in resolving your vanity, but one cannot transform oneself overnight. Your spiritual healing slayed the spirit of your vanity, but there are still traces that cling to you; and stubbornness is one of the telltale signs."

"Padre, may I ask you a personal question?"

"You may."

"What secret did you learn about mankind?"

"The secret that I learned took my whole life to learn. It wasn't until the last few days of my life that it all began to make sense to me. I suffered for Jesus and my fellow man, and in my suffering I learned to be humble; and in my humility I saw the divine self of my fellow man."

"Did you suffer because man was blind to his own divine nature? Because man could not see that he was divine in essence, did this knowledge add to your suffering?"

"Yes. Immensely. It was very hard to make my fellow man aware of his divine nature; and I used my spiritual authority of the confessional booth to help my fellow sinners (I use that word advisedly) become aware of their divine nature, but it wasn't easy. It was a challenge to find the gold treasure underneath all the muck of man's ego. But it was a challenge I could not refuse, and I gave confessions with an open heart."

"You know, I may read my book *Healing with Padre Pio* again just to get the feel of what you said to me, because I honestly think that I can learn from our conversations. You said things that took a long time to register, and I think there are things that I haven't quite grasped. Our dialogues here are of a different nature, because there is always the element of doubt that my mind filters what comes through and taints the message; and I guess that's going to always be until I surrender completely to the process. But I don't know if I can do that, because I've been burned once too often by the mind. It is a dangerous place to be, in one's own mind; and few souls find their way to the higher planes of Soul. I guess it's all about trust, isn't it?"

"*Trust in yourself. Don't let this worry you. Just continue what you are doing and let the process take care of itself. If it's not working, I guarantee you the flow will stop.*"

"I doubt that. The mind is endless in its information. It will feed the ego all it needs to inflate it."

"*Yes, but you have a handle on your ego self now. You know when you are being inflated and when you are given information useful to your process. All I am doing is facilitating your process. Whether it is your mind or me doesn't really matter, as long as it helps you in your process.*"

"And how does one know that one is being helped? It could all be one grand delusion, could it not?"

"*Maybe. That's up to you to figure out. Once again, it's all about trust.*"

"Okay. I have to ponder this. I resonate with you, and I know this from my book *Healing with Padre Pio*; so I have to broaden my scope and learn to trust in this process and let Divine Spirit speak freely. Is that it?"

"*In essence, yes. But, as you say, Spirit is One; so when you come right down to it, do you trust yourself enough to continue this dialogue?*"

"I enjoy it. It gives me relief. It helps me cope. It allows for the possibility of growth. It opens new doors for me. It introduces concepts that I am not consciously aware of. It's great to keep the creative energies flowing. I have any number of reasons to continue this process. But I don't want it to become a crutch. I want to use it as a tool of active imagination. This is an effective tool for my creative writing. I just don't want to chat for nothing. That's why I hope every time we talk that something new will appear. Like this morning. I learned something new about suffering, and I thank you."

"*You're welcome. Now, let's end for today; okay?*"

"Okay. Until the next time..."

22. A Dialogue on Depression

Monday, August 18, 2014

"Good morning, Padre. The movie actor Robin Williams died last week. He committed suicide. Apparently he was addicted to drugs and was recently diagnosed with Parkinson's disease, and he suffered from depression for a long time; and now there's a media dialogue going on depression. People who have suffered depression for years are speaking up. I don't feel about depression the way most people do. I'm not sure it's a disease, as they claim it to be; I think it's more psychological than biology based, and I'd like to open up a dialogue with you on this subject. Are you up to it?"

"Yes, by all means. Good morning, my friend. Depression is a disease of the mind; but it is more of a psychological disease than a biology based disease, insomuch that one's personality has the disadvantage of being influenced by the soul's karmic history. This is what you have intuited, and I would concur."

"I don't want to make light of it, because depression is much too serious to simply relegate to bad choices that we've made throughout our many lives that have added up to a dark spot on our soul that we pass onto ourselves from one life to the next, but that's what it comes down to in the end, or so I believe; and I don't think there will be a cure for depression unless the moral character of man is brought into question. As I've always believed, the shadow self is the fundamental issue with depression, but science does not want to go there. Some therapists do, especially Jungian psychotherapists, but on the whole hard science wants to treat depression as a biology-based disease. I know that life tragedies like losing one's job, the death of a loved one, a sudden life-altering illness, or whatever play a major role in throwing one into depression; but I still say that psychology and not biology is the major cause of depression, and I'd like to know what you think. Is it biology or psychology?"

"They affect each other; but primarily, it is the moral character of a person that colors one's personality, and personality attracts to itself the reality that it is best suited for its expansion and growth. It's all about vibrations. One's frequency attracts one's reality—"

"And we can't control our frequency with pharmaceuticals, can we?"

"In effect, we can; but the change does not last. It has to be repeated. This is the root cause of drug addiction."

"Tell me, what is depression? Give me a clear definition, please."

"Depression is a state of mind brought on by one's spiritual state. When a person is unable to take control of his life, he subjects himself to the unresolved aspect of his nature, which psychology calls the shadow self. This unresolved aspect of one's spiritual personality—the karma of one's past lives—will cloud one's personality and pull one down into its unresolved nature, which is the reality of one's non-being, because the shadow is all that soul wants it to be but is not. This is why one feels so utterly hopeless when in a state of depression. And because everyone has unresolved karma, everyone is subject to depression; but it all depends upon the kind of life one is living. Change your frequency, and you change your life. This is where the science should be heading."

"So there may be a way of curing depression through sound therapy, then? By listening to healing music? And by this I mean music that will lift one's vibrations to a higher frequency which does not resonate with the energies of one's shadow personality?"

"Yes. Music therapy is one modality. The right music will change the frequency of one's depression-vibration; but then the person must sustain the frequency by following up on the treatment of building a pattern of behavior that will sustain the

higher behavior so one's higher frequency cannot be overwhelmed by the vibrations of one's unresolved lower nature."

"From everything that I read on depression over the years, I've always gotten the feeling that everyone wants to blame life for causing one's depression, as though life has pushed them into a corner and they have no way of fighting back and depression sets in; but because I've come to believe that life doesn't just happen to us as such, we have to take account of what we have done to be where we are. When I see a homeless person, for example, I ask myself: 'I wonder what his story is?' Because I know that he didn't just land on the streets one day. He got there because of choices that he made along the way. Am I being too hard here, too insensitive?"

"Everyone certainly has their story, and their story is their relationship with life; but, as you say, life just doesn't happen to us. There are many factors that we cannot control, but those we can determine our frequency; and we are always free to change our frequency. But man is not aware of this yet. Not consciously, that is. The science of vibrations is coming to the fore, but it will take time to prove that we can change our behavior by changing our frequency, and that we can change our frequency by the values that we live by. This is the religion of the future, and it is a long way off yet. The old dinosaur religions will take a long time to die off, and the evolution of the new religion/science will depend upon the need. Society is in transition, but it does not know what it wants to become and there is a lot of confusion—"

"Padre, I don't feel our connection this morning. I feel a little bit uneasy about this dialogue. Why is that? Is it you that I'm talking to, or my own mind? Because something doesn't feel quite right."

"It's in how you feel about your personal responsibilities that you have let mount up. They have an oppressive power over you. You can't resolve them all in one day, so just put that thought out of your mind and do one responsibility a day and do the rest another day. That way you won't feel guilty. And speaking of guilt, this is one of the biggest contributing factors to depression—all of

one's hidden guilt comes to the surface in the form of despair. Despair is the feeling of hopelessness, dejection, gloom, anguish, desolation—all feelings that press down on you and keep you in a state of debilitation. Guilt is emotion created when one believes that one has done wrong. If one represses one's guilt and continues to do so, the guilt builds up and clouds one's personality. Depression has just begun to be studied, but it will open the door to the inner self once the connection is made between depression and personality—"

"Psychological connection?"

"Yes. It's much too simple to blame the genes. The genes are affected by the mind, and the mind is affected by the way we live; and unless the connection is made between the way we live and our reality, the issue of depression will never be resolved."

"I've always felt that everyone talks around the subject of depression, never about depression. Sure, they talk about the symptoms of depression—how one feels and all that; but they never seem to address why they feel that way, never really pointing the finger at the real cause of their depression, always skirting it like it's a dangerous tiger they are afraid to face for fear of being swallowed up. Am I anywhere near the truth here?"

"Your book The Lion that Swallowed Hemingway says it all. What swallowed Hemingway if not his own shadow? And who created Hemingway's shadow? He was the author of his own personality, and his personality had a dark side. His dark side was his shadow. Was that caused by life or by Hemingway's way of life? This book speaks to the issue of depression clearly, but it's much too stark a truth for people to acknowledge, because that would mean taking responsibility for one's own personality and one's shadow. This is where the issue of depression should be going. And in many cases it is. But it's a slow process, and science will not embrace this perception for a while yet. It takes science a long time to catch up to the visionaries."

"I can only speak for myself, but I've been subject to bouts of depression which I've never really allowed myself to wallow in because I was driven by my daemon to find my true self—my calling, if you will; but what I've learned about myself is that it's very easy to be pulled into the depths of one's despair if one does not face the reality of one's life. When I heard that voice in my mind that asked me the question 'Why do you lie?' I saw for the first time in my search for my true self that there was a part of me that was false; and that's what fueled my quest for my true self. And I came to the conclusion that self-deception was our greatest threat to personal growth, wholeness, and happiness. That's why I think depression is a disease of the personality and not the mind, as such. The personality is the self we have created, and if it has a dark spot that clouds our reality than we have to do something about it; and the only way we can change our personality is to change the values that we live by. This was my conclusion after years of seeking for my true self. Can you comment on this?"

"I'd be happy to. The values that one lives by determine the nature of one's personality; that is a given. And it is a given also that if one changes the values that one lives by, he will change the nature of his personality. The logic is sound, but it is much too demanding for one to consider. People are creatures of habit, and habits are hard to change. It takes a traumatic experience for one to change his habits. This is why so many people fall into depression. They cannot change their habits. The addict, for example, does not want to give up his habit; that's a big demand. And so life goes on as usual until the weight of the habit becomes too heavy to support and something has to give. That's what happened to the movie actor who took his own life. That's what happens to most suicides. They cannot support the weight of their own shadow, and it destroys them. Sound and light therapy are the new healing modalities, and they will become more acknowledged for their efficacy in good time; but they have to be followed up with behavioral therapy, because unless one changes one's behavior he will fall back into the same pattern, and that's what caused his problem in the first place. When all is said and done, one has to take responsibility for one's life; that's the

ultimate cure for depression, because karma is a personal responsibility."

"Now you're sounding very harsh. That's not like you, Padre."

"It is me. I just don't want to coddle the truth."

"Good. I like that. This opens the door to a theme that has concerned me my whole life—the issue of authenticity. I'm not quite sure how to go about this, Padre; but because I feel it is not only related to the issue of depression but is central to it, I want to explore this issue of authenticity. When I heard that voice in my mind when I hit a brick wall in my search for my true self (I was sitting in my basement bedroom of our family home, and I was in my middle twenties and had started to live Gurdjieff's teaching) ask me the question 'Why do you lie?', I was stunned. Not just because I heard a voice in my mind for the first time in my life, but because the voice asked me why I lied; and this led to my life-long quest for authenticity, which came to happy resolution in my spiritual healing with you that became the inspiration for my novel *Healing with Padre Pio*. Even though I felt that I was authentic—and which I paid a very dear price to realize as I lived Christ's teaching of 'dying to my life to find my life'!—I didn't realize how inauthentic I still was until I came upon you—the Saint of Humility! And you slew my vanity with such gentle ease that I barely saw it coming; and now I am less vain and more authentic, I feel that I have enough authority to speak about inauthenticity and depression, because I cannot disassociate the two. I honestly believe that the root cause of depression is the issue of one's false nature, or one's inauthentic self—which comes right back to one's shadow. But it's much more complex than this, because one's shadow speaks to one's past lives as well. In a word, Padre; I've come to believe that depression is a state of mind in which one's soul is trapped in the false nature of one's non-being. This sounds so metaphysical, but when one has been through the transformation of one's nature from the false to the real—one's non-being to one's being—one does not relegate the experience to metaphysics or psychology: it is real! And I know the price that I paid for my reality. Dying to one's life to find one's life is not philosophy or psychology; it's a way of life in which one shifts one's priority of serving one's selfish ego to a new priority of unselfish living, which transforms one's consciousness from that of being and non-being to one that is both being and non-being, as I did; and this third entity is one that is neither one's being nor one's non-being, but both: it is the birth of one's Soul. This is the 'new creature' that St. Paul talked about. It is the spiritual rebirth that Jesus talked about. It is the 'new man.' I experienced this, Padre; and I know that you did also. That's why you said that we were the same. We took a different path, but we ended up in the same place—the realization that Soul is who we are. Have I gone too deep here? Because it is all related—"

"It is all related, and you have not gone too far. You have expressed yourself clearly, and I would like to respond. Yes, depression is related to our false sense of self. It is that state of consciousness where one's center of gravity, or one's 'I' is trapped in one's false self, as you have correctly deduced; and the only way to liberate oneself from this state of mind is to take responsibility for shifting one's 'I' back to one's genuine self. This is what the problem with the issue of depression is all about. You see it, I see it; but the world is blind to this reality, because the world wants an easy solution to man's oldest problem—the problem of man's salvation. Depression is a private hell, and the only way out of hell is forgiveness for one's sins—if I may be allowed to use such old and outdated language, though it does make the point rather nicely; and by forgiveness I mean the penance that one must do to transform the consciousness of one's depression. When I gave my penitents forgiveness in my confessions, I directed them to change their ways. The penance that I gave them was to remind them to change their ways. This can be called behavioral modification, as we referred to before; but whatever we call it, one has to change one's ways if one wants to overcome depression. It's not enough to take pills and talk to a therapist; one has to change one's behavior, because in the effort to change one's behavior one transforms the consciousness of one's depressed self—the identity of his

depression, if you will. Once a depressive does not mean that one will always be a depressive. It's not like they say about the alcoholic, that he will be an alcoholic for life even after he stops drinking; that's an incorrect evaluation of the experience. One is what one is for all time at the time that one is what one is, because NOW is the only reality. So changing one's depressive self can only happen when one changes one's life NOW. Pills may help give one the energy and incentive, but only behavioral modification can transform the consciousness of the depressive to the non-depressive. Does that help answer the question for you?"

"Not quite. I don't think I made myself clear on what it means to be trapped in one's false self. I know that I was. And this was confirmed for me by my unconscious with the poem that I wrote in high school called 'Noman' that came to me in a bombastic burst of inspiration. I was Noman; but it took me years to realize that Noman was my archetypal false self, the false self of every personality that I had created in the history of my life on Earth; and it was my destiny in this life to liberate myself from the consciousness of my false self. And that's what my journey of the self was all about—"

"And mine, if you don't mind my interruption. Yes, you are on the right track here; but bear in mind just how deep this is. This goes to the issue of man's purpose in life and the whole process of man's evolution. You have managed to cut to the very quick of the human condition, and whether anyone can make any sense of it or not will remain to be seen; but I for one admire how you managed to transform the consciousness of your false self through your own intuitive efforts and indomitable spirit. You said that you would find your true self or die trying, and you have succeeded; and now you want to elaborate on this issue of authenticity because you feel there is more to be said?"

"Yes. Ever since my spiritual healing I've been different. I've thanked you once and twice and three times for my spiritual healing, because it changed my life in a way that nothing ever could had I continued on my path, and I'm not sure I would have shed my vanity had I not met you through my medium; but even so, I continue to shed more subtle layers of vanity every now and then, like I did last week and which I recorded in my spiritual musing 'Cricket in My Window,' so I want to make the point as clear as I can that depression is much more insidious than people think—because it goes to the very core of their non-being. In other words, what I am saying is that when one falls into depression one has trapped themselves in the depths of one's false nature, which is the non-being of one's process of becoming. Once again, this is abstract and metaphysical; but how else can one talk about the natural process of one's individuation through the enantiodromia of life?"

"One can speak in metaphor and symbols and allegory, but when you strip it all down it comes to what you have said: depression is a state of consciousness that has trapped one's inner self in the unresolved consciousness of one's non-being; and the only way out is to resolve it through behavior modification, as you did with Gurdjieff's teaching and Christ's sayings. That's why you speak with authority of the subject of depression. You have lived through it."

"And why I say that people don't want to address the real issue of depression, because it means pointing the finger back to oneself. It just seems to me that people like to be victims. Being a victim of depression draws sympathy, and people are so hungry for sympathy that they can't shift the blame from the world to themselves; or am I being too judgmental?"

"The truth can be harsh, and it can be very judgmental because the truth sees both sides and must choose which is right. Both sides are right, of course; but the reality of the non-partisan truth passes judgment on both sides. The individual is responsible for his own life, despite the part played by life. Life is responsible in many ways, but the individual would be wrong to blame life for his condition. The man who got laid off from his job and blamed life for falling into depression was not being honest with himself. Losing his job affected his personality, so life played a role in his depression; but ultimately it was the nature of his personality that pulled him down into depression, and had he the wisdom to

transform his personality in a way that offset his depressive self,
he would have spared himself his own death by suicide. I'm of
course referring to the article you read in the paper yesterday
about the male nurse who was laid off from his job and spiralled
into depression. This is a common experience, and the end result
is not always the same; it all depends upon how one deals with the
situation. As you have come to see, it all comes down to how we
live our life. Life really is a journey of the self, and no two journeys
are the same."

"This is a touchy subject, because who wants to be told that
their life is a lie? I did that once in a letter to my brother. He
hasn't spoken to me since. And when I do it in my writing,
people take offense. One friend said, 'I don't feel safe anymore'
after she recognised herself in one of my musings. It's like the
light shone on her, and she didn't like what she saw, and now
she wants nothing to do with me. So what's one to do, Padre?
You did say, and I quoted you for my novel *Healing with Padre*
Pio, 'Hypocrisy is the greatest evil of our time. It exists in all
levels of our society, in high places and in low places.' It's okay
then to see someone else's hypocrisy, but we don't want anyone
pointing out our own; do we? That's why you were so gentle with
me when you brought me face to face with my own vanity. God,
what an experience! I still can't thank you enough for my
spiritual healing; but that's not the way the rest of the world
feels about their vanity. They don't want to give it up. And this is
why the world is what it is; right?"

"It is the enantiodromia of life; and yes, people do not want to
see their own vanity. This was my biggest challenge. We have
covered much ground here today. I think we should save the rest
of this discussion for another time, when you are fresh with new
thoughts and energy. I'm happy that you opened up the issue of
depression. It needs a good airing."

"If you don't mind, I'd like to share an impression that I've
been having lately that I have a much better sense of just how
trapped a soul can be in the consciousness of their
inauthenticity; and this throws a whole new light on how I see

people now. But thank God I no longer judge them as I used to, because I am now very conscious of the enantiodromiac nature of the individuation process; which is why I said to Penny yesterday, I don't see things in black and white anymore. Everything is a shade of grey. So I don't judge people, Padre; because I know that they are both their false and true self, and always in a state of becoming. I have learned to accept people for what they are; but, I hate to say this, now I have developed an instant dislike for some people because I see them only too clearly!"

"It's like the fruit of the tree. Some you enjoy because they are ripe and taste good, and some you don't enjoy because they are not ripe enough and don't taste so good. We all have those feelings about people. Your feelings are more sensitive than most people. That's what writers have, though; and because they have these sensitivities, they unveil life for the rest of us to see. This is why you should get back to your stories—"

"Point taken. Thank you. Until next time..."

23. A Volcano of Anxiety

Tuesday, August 19, 2014

"Good morning, Padre. I'm in trouble. I feel like I'm about to explode. I feel like a volcano of anxiety, and I need your help. Can you help me, please?"

"I've been waiting for you to ask me. Yes, of course I can help. It's been a long time coming, but now you must face the reality of your return to the town that dishonored you with their rebuff of your book. You opened the eyes of that community, and the price you and Penny paid was very steep; but that part of your journey is over and now you must reconcile with your community, and you fear this reconciliation. But it must be done. Not that you have dishonored your community, friends, and family; you honored them with the truth, but they did not realize this for many years. Now they do, since you have published many books since and they see that you were not what they thought you were. Your anxiety will dissipate as you work your way up north, and it will be gone by the time you return back home; but in the meantime you must learn to not let the fear of returning to your hometown burden you. It is not good for your heart, and I have to keep an eye on you to keep you safe. Yes, my son; I will help you. We have much work to do together. This is the beginning of another journey into the Heart of God. You have been included in the inner circle, and I welcome you into my understanding of the secret knowledge—"

"Let's hang tight, Padre. I don't need any stroking. I've come too far for this kind of ego-massaging. All I'm asking is that I don't blow a gasket, because I think that could easily happen. I am so anxious that I've thrown Penny into a fright, and that's the last thing I want to do. I love her, and I want to spend the last few years of our life as free of anxiety as possible, and I am asking for your help because you understand me better than I understand myself. I just finished reading the last two transcripts of our sessions together in my book *Healing with Padre Pio*, and I feel really close to you this morning; so, please, no molly-coddling. I want to be honest and fair and up front with you, and I never thought I'd feel this way, but I am asking for your help like I would have when I was a child praying to God to help me. God, what vanity still! Is there no end to it? Must I continue to be humbled? Even in my request for God's help I cannot help but see that vanity still stands between God and me; what am I going to do, Padre? What did you do? I see from my second last session with you that you did not experience humility until just a few days before your death; must I have to wait to die before I can experience humility too?"

"*No. You have already earned the privilege of the greatest virtue of them all, the humble spirit of the man who sees his own soul. I am not coddling you, my son; I am concerned for your welfare. You are precious to me. We have come a long way together. You have a lot more to give before you cross over, and it is imperative that you stay healthy. Anxiety is a silent killer, and I'm glad you asked for my help. I cannot intervene without your permission, and now that I have it I beseech the Almighty God on your behalf. Be patient, my son; I see it all before me now, and it will all be for the good. There is no harm in your path, and all will unfold according to the grace of God. Go about your business as if it were just another day, and the day will unfold with no harm in your way.*"

"I thought of writing a story on my experience of going back to my hometown, and the title has already come to me: *We May Be Tiny, But We're Not Small*. This will be the story of why Penny and I had to leave my hometown after I published my first two novels. I think writing this novel may work out my anxiety and keep me from exploding. I hope so!"

"*This is your next big project. Yes, it will dissipate your anxiety, and you must begin writing it before you leave. Write the first chapter or two to get you into the flow. This will begin the process of your reconciliation with your community. You have only to begin to initiate your own healing.*"

"It's been almost eleven years since Penny and I left my hometown, and now I have to go back and deal with my emotions. My novel *What Would I Say Today If I Were to Die Tomorrow*? caused such a fuss that it turned the whole town against Penny and me, and it's time to go back. We have to go back to attend to our triplex, but that's the necessary excuse to attend to my repressed feelings for my hometown. That's why I feel like a volcano about to explode, and why I am asking for your help. There are moments when I feel like I just can't hold it in anymore, and I fear what might happen. I hope the idea for this new novel will help calm the savage beast of my anxiety."

"It will. You have only to initiate the process. Begin and you will see how much better it will make you feel. I promise you!"

"Last night sitting in my recliner in front of the TV watching whatever program was on but feeling sorry for myself I felt tears come to my eyes for all the regrets I have in my life and I wanted to crawl into a hole and die; but that would be the coward's way out, and I suffered my anxiety with that same stubborn pride that I have lived my whole life. Why cannot I admit to myself that I could have been a better person? That I could have attended to my personal responsibilities for survival much better than I did? Maybe I do realize it. Maybe that's why I feel so anxious. Because I didn't do what I feel I should have done and I feel this way and there's not a damn thing I can do about it now but wallow in self-pity! God, what a fool I've been!"

"We all make decisions that we later regret, but when we make them we cannot see the consequences; only later do we realize how foolish we were. Why beat yourself up for something you have no control over? That decision was made, and you have regrets now for making it, and you paid the price; so why flog yourself with your regret? It's not necessary. Start fresh. I know it's an old cliché, but starting fresh is always the way to go because there is no other way to unburden yourself of your anxiety. Once again, it's all about vanity. You can see it now, and that's a good thing to know; because now that you see that you feel stupid for what you did and feel humiliated, you can shed yourself of the guilt of your

bad decisions and forgive yourself and start fresh. That's what I always told my penitents when I heard their confessions. I forgave them in the name of Jesus and sent them on their way to start fresh. If I may take the privilege, I forgive you in the name of your Creator and I implore you to go out into the world and start fresh. This much I can do for you, and more because of my love for you. Remember our agreement: we have much work to do."

"Our agreement on the other side?"

"Yes, and over here which we made during your sessions with me."

"Anything to get my mind off my anxiety!"

"On the contrary. I want you to get your anxiety off your mind. That's the whole point of this exercise. You must unburden yourself of your anxiety, and writing a new novel would be a great place to start. Call your Muse. Implore your Muse. Beg your Muse. Just do it!"

"Okay. I'm going to start it this morning. I'm going to go downstairs and get a cup of coffee and then I'm going to open a new file and begin writing the story which I hope will become my novel We May Be Tiny, But We're Not Small. I don't know if I should write this as straight autobiography or a novel memoir. I think it will be a novel memoir. What do you think?"

"I think you should be consistent. Your other novels are fiction based upon your life. I think it would be natural to continue in the same vein."

"I do too. I hope that you are right, that this project will help to dissipate my anxiety, because I don't want to blow a gasket. I don't, for Penny's sake. I could never do that to her. Please, Padre; implore the Almighty on my behalf and let's get this show on the road. It's been a long time coming!"

"No, it hasn't. You had to come to this point. Like I said in our sessions, you have to be in a place of understanding to be in agreement with yourself; only then will one be ready for a spiritual healing. You had to wait all of this time and write all of your books to come to an understanding that will bring agreement with yourself. Now you are ready to write your book. You weren't ready *before, because you weren't ready to deal with it. You have to now. This was brought upon you by life, and life always wins out. Just go with it, and let the chips fall where they may. Okay?"*

"You do amuse me, Padre. Yes, okay; I will go with it and let the chips fall where they may. There is a nice feeling that comes with this kind of abandonment; that's why you said it, didn't you?"

"You have your ways and I have mine. But the important thing is that we understand each other. Go and get your coffee and start your story!"

"I will. Thank you for listening to me..."

P.S. " Penny asked me to ask if you would find us a buyer for our triplex in my hometown. We want to sell it and absolve ourselves of that responsibility. We have two more years of savings before things get really tight, and if we sell our triplex we wouldn't have to suffer the anxiety of economic pressure. Would you look into this for us, please?"

"Yes, of course. Just go and do what you have to do and let God take care of the rest. You are in God's hands now. I promise everything will turn out as you would like. I do not make this promise lightly."

"Thank you."

24. Dialogue on Fear

Wednesday, August 20, 2014

"Good morning, Padre. I have to ask you a question: is most of my fear imaginary? I ask this question because I'm getting very tired of being afraid of something that may never happen. Can you speak to me about fear?"

"*Let me begin by wishing you a good and happy and peaceful day, that it may bring you the inspiration that will motivate you in your journey through life. Now, about fear. In my experience as a Capuchin monk and Holy Confessor, yes; I came to see that most fears are imaginary. This is the nature of the lower self, to be afraid of life. Life is not easy at the best of times, and one will always be in doubt as to its outcome; so fear is a natural consequence of being alive. But man is blessed with the gift of imagination, which has a way of compounding one's fears. It is to the nature of the mind to use imagination in this way, not because it wants to terrorize the self with fear, but because the mind has a tendency to blow things out of proportion. Why?*"

"Yes, why? But let me ask you first: is the mind independent of Soul, our spiritual self?"

"*Yes and no. The mind is the thinking part of soul, and therefore not independent; but the mind is animated by the ego, the self of our lower nature, and our lower nature acts as if it is independent of Soul. It is not, as you have come to realize. So the mind is at ego's disposal, and whatever drives the ego will drive the mind. Ego is driven by its desire to be, and this applies in every aspect of one's life, always seeking to fulfill itself; and whatever ego imagines will impede its fulfillment will create fear. In the simplest terms possible, fear is ego-driven; and the more emphasis one places on the objects of one's desire—be they what they may, like financial security, love, success and whatnot—the more one fears not realizing them. The way to rid oneself of fear is to not*" *place so much importance upon the objects of one's desire. I know this is like asking one to jump over the moon, but it does give one an insight into the causes of fear. Remember this: FEAR IS EGO-DRIVEN."*

"So loss drives one's fears, then? The more one thinks or imagines that one may lose the objects of one's desire, the more fear sets in?"

"Yes. Loss inspires fear. And imagination has a way of creating all kinds of ways to lose what one wants and desires; so the trick is to get a grip on one's imagination and not let it distort the reality of the situation. This of course is very hard to do, because we can't help but think about losing what we need to satisfy our desires; but the practice of detachment is needed to counter the negative effects of our dread of loss. Whenever fear gripped me, I prayed the rosary to take my mind off my fear. I never confronted my fear until the dead of night when it came to me in full force, and then I had to wrestle with my demons until I realized that I was wrestling with myself. It took me a long time to see that my fears were the soul of my inner demons. Face your fears and you will destroy your demons. This is the hard part of the journey of the self, but with enlightened understanding one can make the struggle less difficult. Ask yourself this question whenever a fear possess you: Where do you come from? Then wait and see what answer you get. Chances are that it will not reply, because it does not want to admit that fear is not real. It is the imaginary part of you that you created from your desire. The thought of not realizing your desire gave birth to your demon of fear, and if you let go of your attachment to your desire then your demon-fear will disappear. It has no choice, because it's not real."

"I've been reading *Healing with Padre Pio* because I want to get back the feeling of being with you like I was in my spiritual healing sessions with the medium who channelled you, and it does give me heart because I get to re-experience the spirit of my inspiration; and I guess what I'm trying to say to you this morning is that fear has a way of crushing one's spirit. It has a way of sucking the life force out of me, and this pulls me deeper into what I dread to call depression. This is why I suppose I initiated these dialogues. I want to recapture that energy of inspiration that I always get whenever I'm working on a new book. I fear the loss of inspiration, Padre."

"All of man's demons are first cousins. They are all born of the same soul, and when one has one fear one invites the whole family. This is why it's important to face your fears one at a time. When you face one fear, you face them all; but by facing one fear at a time, it doesn't seem so threatening. Take your fear of going up north to your hometown. Once you face this fear you will have faced all of the demons that are related to this one demon, and they will lose their power over you. The problem with facing one fear is the dread of loss; that's why it has the power it has. Fear gets its power from our desires. Once again, fear is ego-driven. Ego is all about one's desire to be fulfilled, however this fulfillment may come—by way of love, money, success; so inevitably the more value we place on the objects of our desire, the greater our fear will be when we think we may not realize them. This is central to Buddhist thought. That's why they place so much value on the art of detachment. Detach yourself from your desires and you take away the power of your demons."

"But we can't live without desire. Desire is to man what air is to life. We live to realize our desires. This is what drives every person—the desire to be a singer, a poet, an artist or a doctor. How can we live without desire?"

"We cannot. But we can learn to not be slaves to our desires. Who is in control of your life: you, or your desire?"

"I follow that. But what about one's calling? Like the calling to write a book? When I'm called, I obey. This is the only way I can satisfy my calling. I am not in charge of my calling. My calling is in charge of me."

"Yes and no. One is always free to choose. When you choose to listen to your calling, then you are working in conjunction with your calling; but when you let your calling take over your life, then you are in danger of letting your desire take over your life, as many people do, and this opens you up to all the fears that may

come with the thought of failure. It's always six of one and half a dozen of the other. This is the eternal struggle of life, and the driving force of what you have come to realize as the enantiodromia of life."

"I'm thinking of Robin Williams, the movie actor who recently took his own life. His dread of loss must have been enormous to drive him to the despair of suicide. I've had thoughts of letting go, but never to that extent; but what I want to know is if depression is born of one's dread, which is born of one's ego's desire for fulfillment. Does that make any sense to you?"

"It makes perfect sense. As I said, FEAR IS EGO-DRIVEN. *Depression is an insidious state of mind. I hesitate to call it a disease, but there is no other word to explain it; so let's call it a disease of the mind. And since the mind is animated by our lower self, it is ego-driven; which means that depression is an ego-related disease. This is why it's vital for a person suffering from depression to get out of himself, to go out and be with people and get involved with life; because the more you give of yourself to the life process, the more ego will fulfill itself. It's the fear of not fulfilling oneself that fuels one's depression. The movie actor who killed himself suffered from the pressures of his career. The fear of failure drove him to despair because he could not sustain his ego's need for fulfillment. It was a terrible cycle that he created, and he didn't know how to get off the wheel of his own life until it spun out of control."*

"Now that you mention it, fear of failure has created a demon in me that plays havoc with my life. I fear that my time is running short and I will not get the recognition that I desire for my writing. So if I let go of my desire for acknowledgement, you're saying that I would take away my demon's power?"

"Yes. Your fear of never being recognized for your writing talent has created a nasty demon, and the only way to face this demon is to get more involved in getting your books recognition. Until then, it's a false fear."

"I want to be very honest with you here. I think I have something special to give to the world in my writing. I don't think just anybody can write a book like *Healing with Padre Pio*, or *The Golden Seed*, or *The Lion that Swallowed Hemingway*; these books were born of a specific perspective on life, one that is not easily come by. Why, then, if I may ask, does not the divine law of synchronicity assist me in getting these books the recognition that I think they deserve—because I've come to see that this divine law has come into play into the lives of most successful people in the world? Why not me?"

"You do make me smile. Now you want to blame God for your lack of success, is that it? But I do see what you mean. Of course, success does not come by itself. There are many factors involved. One does one's part, and then the law kicks in to assist one; that's the way it's always been. The law has kicked in for you to get you to the place where the law of synchronicity has to kick in, but you have to assist it by making the effort to get your books out there. Place yourself in a position to be helped. That's the short answer. The long answer is that God has bigger plans for you. You can't see them, and this plays havoc with your desire to be acknowledged as a writer. But both will come together in short order, as long as you commit yourself to getting your books out there. Why not give it a try and see what happens?"

"If I may be my contrary self for a moment, I have a blog that gets my books out there. Is that not public venue enough? I know I could do more, and I intend to; but many people have seen my blog, couldn't one of these people be someone that could make it happen for me, or am I dreaming?"

"Dreaming is good. Yes, you are getting your writing exposure, but you have yet to connect with the right person. Just keep doing it, and do more to get your books to publishers. You can't be in the game if you don't bring your cards to the table. Bring your cards to the table. Show them what you got."

"I can't argue with that logic, not that I want to argue. I notice in these dialogues that you are much more forthright than in my spiritual healing sessions. You were very gentle with me back then. Have I grow up since?"

"Considerably. This was due to your commitment to write and solve the mystery of your parallel life. The effort you put into your writing freed you from the forces that kept you in the dark about yourself. Life is always giving us opportunities to grow, and because you have a commitment to understanding life through your writing you have grown considerably since our spiritual healing sessions. This is good. I can speak a little more freely with you now."

"But not freely enough to let me know just how independent you are from me, that you are not a product of this process that I have covered under the forgiving tent of 'active imagination'? I am delighted when fresh thoughts come through, like your comment that fear is ego-driven; but it's not quite convincing enough yet. I need further convincing. Is this forthcoming, or am I dreaming again?"

"Trust the process. Don't think about whether I am a product of your own mind or independent of your mind; that only filters the process. Let it be and let the thoughts come freely. The thoughts will speak for themselves."

"Do you remember in my spiritual healing sessions when you said that it wasn't meant for me to do this sort of thing; that I said I couldn't trust my mind enough to involve myself in this kind of communication and you said that it wasn't meant for me to go this way? Well, this is what I'm doing now."

"That was then, this is now. You have become much more independent of mind because of all the books you have written since Healing with Padre Pio, and you can indulge in the practice of 'active imagination' without fear of being pulled into the fantasy world that you indulged in before when you tried to fulfill your ego desires through imaginary scenarios. You know the difference now, and you're not easily fooled. Just continue trusting yourself. And, by all means, question whatever comes through. This is the way it should be."

"I have to ask. Don't you get tired of my equivocating? All of my moaning and groaning? My prevarications?"

"If I said yes, it would be lying; but I will not allow myself that state of mind because it's not in my job description—"

"Good one, Padre! So, how do you put up with me, then?"

"Actually, because you are aware of your prevarications you make my job a lot easier. You wouldn't believe some of the things I have to put up with to get one to the point where you are now. Life is a challenge, and I respect the human condition in all of its enantiodromiac nature. What else can one do?"

"I guess the journey is all about individual steps, not giant leaps; and with every step we take we inch our way closer to where we are destined to be, so I appreciate your patience with me. But it is hard. What I would love is for some uplifting experience to jumpstart my life so I can re-engage with my inspiration and get my life back on track; would that be possible?"

"Yes; but it would be much more certain if you jumpstarted your own life by not prevaricating as much as you do. Take on one job at a time and do it to the end, and then take on another, and another; and you will be amazed at how inspired you will be— because DOING is the energy that feeds the spirit of inspiration, and the more you do the more you will be inspired."

"This is my beef with spiritual paths: they give us the formula in a few words (such as the sayings of Jesus), and the rest is all about DOING. But we never tire of looking for the MAGIC FORMULA that will solve all of our problems, as though there is one magic formula; that's why we are never satisfied. But because I know there is no magic formula but DOING, I am burdened by the weight of this realization, and I prevaricate!"

"I couldn't agree more. This makes you a special case, and one I enjoy working with. If we could only get you to break through to the other side of your prevarication, you would see just how free you really are. But that will take time, and patience, and a lot of commitment on your part to overcome the static energy of your procrastinating habit. You do put things off, you know!"

"And I use my writing as a refuge for my procrastination. But look at all the books that I have written, despite my lazy habit!"

"As I said, it's always six of one and half a dozen of the other. But you can have both, you know. It's all a matter of initiative and organization. Apply your initiative to DOING and organize your time more efficiently."

"Point taken. Thank you for the dialogue on fear. It's opened me up to hope, one of your favorite virtues if one may call hope a virtue—"

"You may, and it is the one virtue that keeps the door open for new possibilities. Without hope life would be very depressing. Perhaps one day when you have more energy we can dialogue on hope, if you so desire."

"I know that hope was very high on your list. I have a book called *Pray, Hope, and Don't Worry, True Stories of Padre Pio*; so I know how much value you placed on hope. I opened this book up just now and read a few lines and this jumped out at me: 'Even as a youth, Padre Pio understood the transcendent value of suffering. He once said, 'If humanity could realize the value of suffering, they would ask for nothing else.' And you are quoted as saying to your spiritual director Father Benedetto Nardella, 'My sufferings are more precious to me than gold.' This is why I jumped with joy when Carl Jung ended his iconic *Red Book* with the words that Jesus gave to Philemon: 'I bring you the beauty of suffering. That is what is needed by whoever hosts the worm.' And by worm, I take Jesus to mean man's dark side; because through suffering we transform the 'worm' and realize our spiritual self. That's why I understood you so implicitly, Padre. I understood your way of the cross, because I had also experienced the joy of self-transformation through suffering; and I loved my spiritual healing sessions with you because you are so rich in the consciousness (and consequent joy) of suffering that it was like drinking in the sacred waters of truth when I listened to what you had to say about my situation. Your truth healed me, Padre. The joy of your suffering healed me. The compassion of your suffering healed me. The humility of your suffering healed me. I couldn't get enough of you. Perhaps this is why I initiated these dialogues—"

"There are many reasons, and yes; the main reason is because we have a meeting of minds on the spiritual benefits of suffering."

"I don't know if it's ever going to happen, but I did get inspired to write a book called The Beauty of Suffering. God, I'd love that book to happen; but time marches on, and I don't know if it will."

"Yes, it will happen. It will be a short book, like your book Why Bother? It will be inspired by Jung, but you will expound upon the transformative nature of suffering. It will be an extraordinary achievement. I look forward to it very much. It will be a few years down the road yet, but it will be written."

"Suffering as a spiritual path is so out of context with today's world that I don't ever see this concept taking off. Because if it were so, *Healing with Padre Pio* would be more widely read, and *Why Bother? The Riddle of the Good Samaritan.* Even good Christians don't want to think about suffering as a gateway into heaven. They want God to remove their suffering, little realizing that suffering is God's gift to man. The irony is too much to bear. If it is for me, how much more burdensome for you—"

"I don't see it as ironic. I know how difficult life can be for some people, and the spiritual value of suffering is seldom realized while one is in the throes of suffering; but later, if one has time to think about it, one will see the spiritual benefits; and one may even experience the joy. It is ironic, of course; but from my place of all knowing and seeing, there is no irony. There is only what is, and what is includes all meanings. Nonetheless, this does not diminish the literary value of a book called The Beauty of Suffering. Literature is a gateway to greater understanding, and your book will go a long way to helping people see suffering in a new light, the way Jesus intended for suffering to be understood and appreciated. That's why he died on the cross for mankind. He suffered to dignify the human experience."

"That's a good note to end on. Thank you, Padre."

"You're welcome, my friend."

25. And the Rains Came Down

Thursday, August 21, 2014

"Good morning, Padre. The rains came down yesterday. I had just finished laying the sod in the gully between our yard and the road, which I did to keep the rain from washing the topsoil; but the rains came down with such fury that the water got under the sod and washed the topsoil into the gully and I have my work cut out today to straighten it all out again. But for some reason, I have a feeling that the rains came down for a reason. And speaking of rain, it has just begun to rain again. I can hear it on the roof. Tell me, am I correct in my intuition that the rains came down yesterday to cleanse the negative energy and impurities in our area, or am I dreaming?"

"No, you are not dreaming. When it rains, it rains for a reason other than the atmospheric changes. When an area is in need of the water of living truth, it rains; there are many levels of vibration to each individual experience. You are a force that attracts the energy of God, and the energy of God interrupts the energy of man; and so it rains to purify the air. Now, good morning. Are you feeling a little better about going up north to your hometown?"

"Yes, I am. Thank you. I've been reading the book about your life and some of the many miracles attributed to you, *Pray, Hope, and Don't Worry* by Diane Allen, and I'm beginning to feel again the sanctity of your life; and I have to say, I'm feeling a little ashamed again for my presumption. I'm glad to be reminded of your devotion to Jesus and the Blessed Mother, and although my old faith has been greatly edified thanks to my spiritual healing with you, and I am still devoutly ensconced in my own relationship with the divine, I'm greatly honored to be dialoguing with you, whose sanctity was realized in your love for Jesus and the Holy Mother. I feel privileged once more, and I don't know how to express the feelings that have been awakened in me. But it is what it is, and I would like to ask you something about my writing."

"By all means, ask. And thank you for your kind words. It does the heart good to be reminded now and then of our place in the world, and your reading of my life brings back memories; and I am thankful. It seems like only yesterday I was in San Giovanni Rotondo. But alas, I am here; and my duties have been greatly expanded. Now, your question?"

"You know my question, but I will ask just to get it on record. You said in one of my spiritual healing sessions that my writing was different, that I was writing from a different perspective. Those weren't your exact words, but the gist of what you said was that my take on life was different, a new way of thinking, and this was creating a need in society; may I ask, what need?"

"The need for understanding. Your perspective has the advantage of being from the neutral state of consciousness that is arrived at when being and non-being become one in a new realized self; and this new self offers the miraculous understanding of the mystical union of the polar opposites. This is why your writing has the effect it does on readers. The power of the living truth washes like the heavy rains in the books you write, and the reader is left wondering why they feel as they do after reading you. Take the member of your spiritual community who could not finish reading Healing with Padre Pio; she could not suffer the integrity of your living truth. It was too much for her, and it threatened her sense of being. And to protect herself, she stopped reading your book; but all the same, she was awakened to a new sense of truth, one that her mind refused to entertain. That's the need that your writing creates—the need for a greater understanding that comes from the mystical union of the lower and higher self that you realized in your quest for your true self."

"The need is there, beneath the surface; but people don't want to give in to this need for greater understanding. I can hear the cries for understanding, but the words are silent; and soul continues to anguish."

"This is the way of the world."

"Padre, I'd like to sleep for a thousand years I feel so tired; what am I to do? As I worked yesterday on my yard I felt the strain upon my body, and I had to rest from exhaustion every ten minutes. My body isn't what it used to be since my open heart surgery, and the memory of what it was cannot accept the reality of what it is; and I long for some relief. I'm in a quandary. And I turn to writing for a refuge; but I don't have the spark of inspiration for a new book yet, and I feel forlorn. I don't want to get into that woe is me state again, that I seem to slip into easily. I know what to do, but I don't have the will to do it; and this fatigues me."

"In short order you will find yourself in a new routine, one that is free of all this worry. You will be free to devote yourself to your life and writing as you have dreamt of doing for years. Trust God. All is as it should be."

"I cannot get over your life as I read *Pray, Hope, and Don't Worry*. Were you that devout in your belief? It overwhelms me!"

"I wish I could have been more devout. Yes, I was that devout; and my love was as deep as I could suffer. You are right to see that we come from a context that is similar but different, but in our difference we understand the mystery of suffering like few others; and in our understanding we can introduce the reader to a deeper perception of life. This is what you are meant to do with your writing. The books you write open the door to this deeper perception, and in time they will find their way to the reader in need of greater understanding."

"Padre, can I ask you about my spiritual path?"

"No. That is between you and yourself. You have a relationship with God that is privileged. Trust your instincts, and let the rest be. In time, it will all become clear to you."

"I know what I have experienced. I trust my own experiences, and I need not take it any further; right?"

"Yes. Just like your experience with the twenty-nine geese. You got the proof you needed to confirm your experience with God. Do you need further proof of your relationship with the Divine?"

"No, I guess not. Sorry for asking. I think I'm just rambling for the sake of talking because I don't really know what to do with myself. I type a little and then read some more of the book on your life just to pass the time, and I feel like I am not being fair to you and myself."

"This is a transition period for you, and one can expect this kind of ambivalence; but it will come to an end shortly. I don't mind spending time with you, regardless of how you feel. Every moment together is precious, both for you and me; and it is not a waste of time. The rains came down yesterday to clear the air for what is to come. Do what you have to do today, and trust God to do the rest. This is the only way to live your life with meaning and purpose."

"I feel like I'm coming back to square one."

"Yes, you are. Square one is the beginning of the end of a long journey, and the day promises new tidings."

"Thank you. I'm going to read now..."

26. Growth and Understanding

Friday, August 22, 2014

"Good morning, Padre. I was up at 3:30 this morning. I couldn't sleep any more, and I couldn't listen to the radio. Too much stuff about the mid-east crisis, all of that madness, so I got up and read some more of *Pray, Hope, and Don't Worry*; and reading all those testimonies about people who experienced you in your holy goodness (not to mention the many miracles attributed to you) made me want to go back to my transcripts of my spiritual healing sessions with you in my novel *Healing with Padre Pio*, and I re-read three or four of our sessions together. God, what a journey that was! Despite feeling that I was right there again with you, I feel so far removed from the self that I was that I have trouble believing that I have come this far. So, once again Padre, I have to thank you for my spiritual healing!"

"*You are more than welcome. If I could show my gratitude for what you have accomplished by way of a sign that would truly impress you, I would; but this is neither the time nor place for that kind of proof—*"

"It's alright. I don't need the proof of your existence. My sessions with the psychic who channeled you were proof enough for me. As to our dialogues, they are their own proof—whatever proof that may be. That's the point I want to make this morning: my belief. You emphasised during my spiritual healing sessions with you that I should always go back to my beliefs, to seek my comfort there; well, I believe we are communicating in our dialogues, but our communication involves the creative dimension of Holy Spirit. Or am I simply trying to validate this by placing it under the all-encompassing tent of God?"

"*Yes and no. It's only natural to have some doubt, but don't let that concern you. What is important is how you feel.*"

"First, I have to tell you that I'm less anxious about going up north to my hometown; and that's good. I'd like to be less anxious, and I would appreciate all the help you can give me. And second; I'd like to make a point about your life in particular and life in general. I'm really enjoying the stories about the effect that you had on people, changing their lives with the holy energy of your sanctified life, and I'm left to wonder: what is the world waiting for? Why all of this nonsense and madness in the world? And then I read what you said in one of my sessions with you in *Healing with Padre Pio*; that life is all about GROWTH and UNDERSTANDING. Which means that it's not so much about the process—because the process varies from day to day; but about the GROWTH and UNDERSTANDING that comes with the process. Correct?"

"*Absolutely. Life will always be life, good, bad, and indifferent; so the process doesn't really matter in the cosmic scheme of things. What matters is the growth and understanding that comes with the process. Life is a journey of the self, and the path the self takes makes no difference because it is all the same path home to God (Divine Spirit is One Path); and it's very comforting that you have embraced this principle, because it makes your life much easier.*"

"May I be allowed a little latitude here?"

"*You may.*"

"I couldn't help but wonder why *Healing with Padre Pio* has not reached a wider audience. There are a lot of Catholics out there. Why are they not attracted to this novel? As I read it again this morning for the umpteenth time, I couldn't help but be impressed by the narrative. It's fascinating! Why has it not found a wider audience? This disturbs me."

"*The narrative is more than fascinating; it's literature of the highest order, if one wants to consider literature as the very best of life experience. And to answer your question, it has not yet found its larger audience because your name has not been profiled yet. Once your name is profiled, all of your books will take off,*" *because each book opens the way for the other; and Healing with Padre Pio will reach a very wide audience one day. I promise you!"*

"As much as I regret my cheekiness with you in my sessions, I love the audacity of my narrator! He pulls no punches with you, and you took it all on the chin! God, what you must have thought of me?"

"How refreshing you were, and still are! Your gift for independent thought is a beacon of light for everyone, and I admire and respect you for having the courage of your convictions. That's the theme you want to discuss with me this morning, though you have difficulty conceptualizing your thoughts—"

"Exactly! I just can't seem to get over how shallow—no, that's not the right word. People aren't shallow, really; they're afraid of life, and in their fear they embrace life with a kind of desperation almost as though in their embrace they will find their salvation; but I can feel their sadness. Am I making any sense to you? Or am I projecting?"

"A little bit of both. Yes, these are difficult times; much more difficult than the world has ever seen, and people are running scared; but this is the cleansing process. It has to be this way for the world to rise above itself. There is no other way to purify the planet of all the negative energy. Man has brought the world to the brink, and it must be brought back. People sense this. This is why there is so much turmoil in the Middle East. The world is being turned upside down over there, because the laws of Spirit have been violated; and it's only natural that life will be thrown into turmoil as chaos has its day. Remember enantiodromia; everything must become its opposite in the course of time. Power has to give way to love, and what is happening is the loss of power and the emergence of love. It is a long and painful process. I believe you used a phrase in one of our sessions. You called it 'the slow burning love of God.'"

"Yes, I did. I love that phrase. I got it from the Inner Master. It speaks to the human condition from a perspective far beyond the average person's comprehension, because it speaks to the law of karma. Suffering is good for the soul, I believe you would have said in your lifetime as the humble Capuchin monk from San Giovanni Rotondo, and perhaps still hold onto that view from over there; but whether you do or not, does not matter. What matters is the GROWTH and UNDERSTANDING that comes with the process; right?"

"It's all about growth and understanding, regardless of what we do in life; and as long as we have an insight into the process of our own life we can embrace whatever comes to us with open eyes. This takes the sting out of life. Now, I believe you have an important thought you want to discuss with me?"

"Several, actually; but I want to begin with what you said about the Jungian concept of enantiodromia—"

"Herodotus, actually. The Greek philosopher inspired Jung with that concept and gave him the insight into the dual aspect of human nature, which became the basis of Jung's understanding of the individuation process. Pardon my interruption. You were saying?"

"I wanted your perspective from your place of all knowing and seeing with respect to Christianity's dogmatic belief in evil. As long as Christianity hangs onto this distinction between good and evil—two separate realities instead of one reality working separately—there will always be this fanatical play of opposites in the world. That's what you believed as a priest of the Roman Catholic Church; but now you are an Ascended Master and have transcended the polar opposites. I guess what I'm asking is this: is the world ever going to come to a better understanding of enantiodromia?"

"In good time. This is the direction of human evolution. You are correct to believe that Jung is still fifty years ahead of his time. His contribution to world thought has not yet begun to be appreciated for his insight into the psyche of man and soul's evolution; but because you have such a meeting of minds with the great psychologist you will be working together to help make this perspective a reality. He is much more of an influence in your life than you realize."

"I gather then that he would love to see my novel *The Waking Dream* out, because he does play a major role in the story?"

"Yes. You will be getting that one out within the next two years. You have a lot of work to do on it to tighten it up and round off Jung's character; but you will enjoy doing it because it will be so rewarding."

"Okay. Another question. As I was reading the stories of your influence in *Pray, Hope, and Don't Worry* the thought came to me—actually, I had just read two or three stories of your miraculous intercessions and I turned to my novel *Healing with Padre Pio* and the thought came to me, very strongly I might add, as though you planted the seed in my mind, to do a You Tube video of each one of my books—in-depth videos that explains the process of each book to give my name the profile it needs to reach a greater audience. Did you plant that seed, or was that just a thought laying around in my mind waiting for me to acknowledge it? Because I got a tingling sensation when the thought popped into my mind, as though I intuitively grasped the significance of what You Tube videos on my novels could do for me—"

"Yes, I planted the thought. It would be a strategically wise move to do a You Tube video on each of your books, starting with your first book after your abortion novel. Those are the books that count, because they speak to the process with a much greater understanding."

"I see my videos getting attention?"

"Yes. Very much attention. Once one connects, the others will follow."

"I see *The Lion that Swallowed Hemingway* connecting."

"Yes. And The Golden Seed. These will be very popular, but your most popular will be—guess?"

"My novel *Healing with Padre Pio*?"

"No. Stupidity is Not a Gift of God. This book will scorch the viewer. The title is so engaging that it alone is worthy of a video."

"That was a tough book to write. But I wrote that when I was still in the throes of anger. It was because I still had a lot of anger in me that I had to clear the air. May I ask why I feel trepidation about *The Lion that Swallowed Hemingway?*"

"Because of his name, which is so highly profiled. But because it is so highly profiled your book will attract attention, and you will offer the reader an insight into this writer's life that other biographers could only hint at."

"Should I be worried?"

"No. That is your demon fear coming out of you. He does have an ugly side that wants to keep you frozen in stasis; but you must never let it worm its way into your mind. You are free to write about your life any way you please, and don't ever let your demon fear possess you again. DON'T!"

"You know all about demon fear, don't you Padre?"

"He was my nemesis."

"And if I'm not mistaken, according to what you said in my spiritual healing sessions, it wasn't until you crossed over that you realized that demon fear was the dark and unresolved side of your own personality?"

"We do create our own demons. Yes, I learned this after I crossed over, and I am delighted to clear the air today. Demon fear is a by-product of our morality; and as long as we believe in good and evil as separate realities, we will always give life to our demon fear. Evil is not separate from man. Man is the author of evil, and only man can resolve evil by transforming it—just as your hero Carl Jung taught with his teaching of individuation."

"Anything else you would like to say this morning?"

"I have enjoyed our dialogue this morning very much. It has laid the groundwork for much more discussion. We will talk again."

"I hope so. I think I'm going to re-read some of the biographies of your life. I feel inclined, because I've noticed that when I read about your life, as I did with *Pray, Hope, and Don't Worry* and my own novel, I feel a lot closer to you, which helps to make a better connection for our talk. I even got a fleeting idea for a novel something like *The Golden Seed* but with you playing the role of the Ascended Master as a major character. Any chance in that?"

"It would be a creative challenge. But we can leave that to Spirit."

"Fair enough. I was just running it by you. But now that the thought has surfaced, will the seed germinate and sprout?"

"As I said, it would be a challenge; but not impossible."

"Alright, no sense pressing the point. I should mention, now that I'm on the subject; what about the thought of sending this book of dialogues to Hay House or some such publisher?"

"It would be fascinating to see what happens."

"But you won't say?"

"Do your own homework, and trust God."

"Fair enough. One more thought before we come to closure. All those miracles and intercessions in *Pray, Hope, and Don't Worry* (I understand there's a second volume out now, which I will have to purchase), plus all of the other little miracles that have been attributed to you that I read in all the other biographies on your life, what does that say about man's dependence upon God for salvation from the miseries of life? Does that not take away from the enlightened understanding of karma and individual freedom?"

"You make a good point; but we've gone over this already. It's not about the process; it's about the spiritual experience that they need to validate their faith. I mediated for my followers, and if God saw fit to heal them, then God healed them. As I said, I was only a humble servant; and my mission was to mediate for those in need of God's assistance."

"Not to labor the point; you did have special graces, which you employed in the service of your mission?"

"Yes."

"So you were more than a mediator?"

"Yes."

"Would you care to elaborate, or do I have to call upon my cheeky self to press the point? After all, what is an Ascended Master anyway?"

"He is one with Divine Spirit. Need I say more?"

"Both mediator and doer, then?"

"Yes."

"And the criteria?"

"Always for the good of soul. Does soul need the healing to firm up one's faith? It's all about GROWTH and UNDERSTANDING. I know what every soul needs to grow in their spiritual nature, and what follows is always for the good of the individual soul. No more, and no less."

"I see a plot forming in my mind for a story with you as the spiritual guide for a soul in crisis. He is going through a dark night of the soul; and the plot unfolds with the appearance of a friendly Capuchin monk who helps the tormented soul out of his distress. How about that?"

"It's a good start. Let it gestate for a year or so. It will come out when it's ready to be sprout. I assure you."

"Padre, I just had a great thought—which was inspired while I was reading *Pray, Hope, and Don't Worry*—about a disaffected Roman Catholic who becomes a seeker and finds the way of all ways and then returns to his Roman Catholic faith! Does that tickle your cockles?"

"Very much. Now you're getting somewhere. You could develop that into a story no less satisfying than your novel The Golden Seed. I would welcome the opportunity to work with you on this novel."

"This would be a what-if? story. What if a seeker who has found the way of all ways and his true self returns to the Roman Catholic faith that he abandoned because he now understands it from an enlightened spiritual perspective that does not contradict the dogmatic limitations of the faith because he understands that it is only another process that leads to GROWTH and UNDERSTANDING. I would love to take on the challenge, not because you would play a leading role; but because of how my narrator would behave going back to his Roman Catholic faith with an enlightened understanding of the Way. Talk about irony! Wouldn't that do wonders for Catholics?"

"Not only Catholics, but for anyone who has lost their faith. Give it to your Muse and see what happens. It will take time to gestate, but the seed has been planted. Just let it be for a while. It'll sprout in its own good time."

"Okay, Padre. I have to go. I'm going to put some bread dough on for focaccia. I'm going to make a simple roasted red pepper and olive focaccia to go with the chick pea minestrone that I made yesterday."

"You bring back memories. I loved my mother's bread. It was one of the few pleasures of my life. I did so enjoy her simple cooking. It always comforted me to eat the food of my peasant village. But, as you know, today this peasant food has become quite fashionable; and that is good."

"Alright. Thank you, Padre. We'll continue this another day..."

27. And So It Begins...

Sunday, August 24, 2014

"Good morning, Padre. Last night I watched the mystic/writer Andrew Harvey interviewed online, and through him I was introduced to the Benedictine monk Bede Griffiths, and I began to do some research on him; and this morning I went on Amazon and looked at some of Bede's books, and as I was reading the idea for my new novel that I mentioned to you yesterday, about returning to the faith after a long and fruitful journey of seeking, popped into my head and I'd like to talk with you about it, if I may?"

"You may. Your research will take you deeper into the teachings of this great master. He invites you into his teaching, and welcomes the idea of your story of a man returning to the faith with an enlightened understanding of the Way. I wish you a good morning, and may the day bring you many blessings."

"First things first. Please, please help me rid myself of this anxiety that hangs about me like a bloody vampire. I'm sick and tired of being anxious. I place myself in your hands. Now: the most important thought that came out of our sessions together when I was writing *Healing with Padre Pio* was what you said to me that **life is a journey of the self**. I resonated with that, because my personal motto was, **life is an individual journey**; and then I read what Jesus said to Glenda Green, **there is only the self and God**, and I had all the confirmation I needed for my belief in the natural process of individuation. I want to elaborate on this concept of the self with respect to the divine Self, because it's my belief that we cannot realize our divine Self unless we make the journey of the self; and this journey is what you have come to call **the process**. Are you following my train of thought?"

"Clearly. This would be the central theme of your new novel; the idea of the process being the—"

"Pardon the interruption, but it just popped into my head that this would be a perfect title for my new novel—*The Process.*"

"Yes. It does capture the central idea very nicely. What then do you wish to explore in this morning's dialogue?"

"I feel that I have covered this ground before, in many ways; but I also feel that there is new and fresh ground to explore in this idea of **the process;** which is why my Muse sprung it on me as an idea for a new novel. I get the feeling that it may be intensely autobiographical, but in an objective kind of way; one that explores the enantiodromiac process on a creatively personal level. Am I headed in the right direction?"

"I could tell you, but it would be more exciting to discover this for yourself, because the creative process, as you know, has its own mind and finds its own way, and it would give your story the excitement of discovery. I can say that the law of synchronicity has begun to work for you, and thoughts and ideas and books and people will come together to help your story take form; and you will have no choice but to write it."

"And so it begins..."

"Yes. And sooner than you expected. Just go with it."

"This is how a new book comes to me; first the idea, then the thoughts, then the little synchronicities, and being introduced to the Benedictine monk Bede Griffiths opened the doorway to the Hindu concept of the divine Self that I need to explore through Griffiths understanding so I can flesh in my protagonist's evolving philosophy of **the process.** I get the feeling that he's going to be like the prodigal son who came back home after a long journey, and there is rejoicing and celebrating by his family; but the irony is that they do not know that he has returned because he understands **the process** and not because of what they think, that he has come back to Jesus to be saved."

"Salvation is always personal, and there are many levels of salvation; but the central theme of your story would be liberation

from the lower self, and this is what Christ's teaching was all about. Given what you have so far, you can develop this concept into a full-fledged novel."

"Okay, the seed is sprouting; but I don't want to go there just yet. I still have a few other projects to get out of the way first. But I will watch and nurture the seed while it is sprouting, because that's how I work my books when they have sprouted and need to grow, and when the time is right I know my Muse will inspire me with my point of entry and I will start writing my story, which I believe is going to be called *The Process."*

"Pay attention to the little signs and coincidences; they will lead you to where you need to go. Now that you have allowed the seed to sprout, you have given permission to the creative spirit to guide you. This is how the process works for you. It works this way for everyone, but always in the context of their individual lives. This is what makes the process uniquely individual but universally the same, because the process is the Way."

"I think I got the central idea for a short story that I've been putting off to complete my series of stories on my spiritual community; and it has to do with the sense of spiritual proprietorship that I sense influences the attitude of the members of this community. I'm hesitant to write it, but I want to make a point that this sense of proprietorship was responsible for a lot of my anger when I woke up to the vanity of my spiritual path; and I would like to set the record straight and clear the air. But I feel some trepidation."

"All of your personal stories make you feel this way, because you are going to be writing from the heart. It's a very difficult path that the honest writer takes when he embarks upon the journey of self-discovery, and your story will be one of self-discovery that will shed light on your relationship with the path you held so dear. Your disappointment with the path was brought about by your spiritual healing, which shed you of the vanity that so defined your relationship with your path and spiritual community; and once you shed your vanity you could no longer abide the attitude of your fellow members, and you became angry, not so much at your

fellow members as at yourself. You hate to be taken for a fool, and now you want to set the record straight. That's a noble purpose. Go for it. I can't wait to read it—"

"Yeah, right! As if you don't already know!"

"I do and I don't. It's all up to you. This is the mystery of the creative process and the reality that it gives birth to. Unless you create it I cannot see it, and I have left that option up to you—"

"That doesn't make sense. You can see what is and what is not from your place of all knowing and seeing; but I won't ask. I think I understand what you're trying to say; that it's better for me to work it out than to ask you what the outcome would be. Is that what you are saying?"

"Yes."

Okay; I have to take on my day. Thank you for our talk this morning. I got the title for my new novel and **my process** has begun!"

"You're welcome."

28. Why Is It So Hard to Forgive Oneself?

Monday, August 25, 2014

"Good morning, Padre. I was doing more research online yesterday and I discovered Ann Baring, the author of *The Dream of the Cosmos: a Quest for the Soul*; she was interviewed by Andrew Harvey. When Ann read the ending of her book I smiled to myself, because she revealed what I had experienced about the individuation of Soul—exactly what we talked about in my novel *Healing with Padre Pio*. At the risk of sounding immodest, this makes my writing cutting edge literature; does it not?"

"Much more than you realize. As I said in our sessions together for your novel Healing, you offer a new way of thinking, a new way of being; and this is as cutting edge as it can be. Now; good morning, my friend. I can feel your anxiety as you approach the day that you leave for your hometown, but don't be anxious; I am with you. Everything will be alright. I promise you."

"I'm sorry I feel so anxious, but I can't seem to help myself. I caught a glimpse of something yesterday as I listened to Ann Baring being interviewed by Andrew Harvey, she was talking about her depression; and something she said gave me a glimpse into my own little bouts with depression. She said that she would break down into tears and didn't know why until she went to a Jungian therapist who worked on her for years, and she became a Jungian therapist in her own right. Well, I've broken into tears a few times for no apparent reason; but I think I know why now. I caught a glimpse that all of my unresolved issues, whatever I have repressed that I did not deal with consciously, presses upon my conscious mind; and rather than burst through, these unresolved emotions affect me, and I cry. I don't realize why I cry, but I think I know why now. I cry out of regret for my life. Can you talk about this, please; because I'd like to get to the bottom of my tears?"

"Yes, certainly. You're understanding of the personality and its repressed shadow side gives you a much greater insight into the nature of depression than most people, and you are right to suspect that your unresolved nature is responsible for the tears that you cry for no apparent reason. There is a tide of emotion in every person, but not all tides have the same depth and power; so some people are affected much more than others. Depression depends upon one's tide of emotion that flows in and out of one's conscious mind like the tides of the ocean, and the cause for why the tides of emotion flow is what concerns the medical doctors and therapists."

"Are you suggesting that there are external factors that affect the tides of emotion responsible for a person's depression, like the moon affecting the tides of the ocean?"

"Yes and no. There are many factors that affect the overwhelming emotions of the human psyche that we call depression; but as powerful as the tide of one's emotions may be, one is always free to float or sink, if I may play upon this image. It's always a personal choice, and it would be wrong to say that one is helpless to the tide of one's emotions."

"What about people who are hit so severely with bouts of depression that they have to stay bedridden for days at a time, and weeks and months even; have they become victims of their unconscious self?"

"Yes."

"Okay. I don't want to pursue this any further today. I got the answer I was looking for with respect to why I cry for no apparent reason, and I'd like to move on to this new area of research that I have fallen into—i. e., the mystic Benedictine monk Bede Griffiths and the Jungian analyst Ann Baring. Why have I been led to these people? Is this where my journey is taking me, into the mainstream with like-minded people?"

"Yes. You can see from the research that you have done so far that the path is all one, but you have given it expression in your own creative way as Andrew Harvey and Ann Baring and Father Bede have done in theirs. It's all good, and your writing will make

a significant contribution to the literature of the Way. Just keep doing what you're doing, following your nudges."

"I hate to say it, but it all comes back to stories, which I've come to believe is the most effective way to transmit the message of the Way; because stories speak the language of image and symbol, which is vastly superior to the expressed rational thought of the mind. When the creative unconscious speaks in images and symbols, it speaks for the whole; which is why I keep getting pulled back to story-writing. This is what I am supposed to do!"

"Everything points to it, and still you keep putting it off. You do like to procrastinate, my friend; but there is an underlying cause. Would you like to know what this cause is?"

"Yes, I would. Perhaps it might give me some peace of mind. At least, I hope so. It's not going to disturb me, is it?"

"No. The cause is past-life related. The regret that you had for not fulfilling your life the first time you lived it affects your parallel life today. Little do you realize just how regretful you were for your first lifetime as Orest Stocco. You fought your own destiny right to the sad end, and you died in that life with so much sorrow and regret that you had to come back to undo what you had done; and here you are today, reliving your same life over again but with an entirely different outcome. You solved the riddle of your life and have broken through to a higher plane, but the memory of your unfulfilled life still haunts you and will continue to do so until you absolve yourself of the guilt you feel for the choices you made the first time you lived your same life. This is not as puzzling as it seems. If you consider your first life as Orest Stocco as just another past life, it will make a lot more sense to you. Because it is the same life, it seems complicated; but it's no less complicated than the history of one's other past lives. Only this time the memory of your past life is so much a part of your current parallel life that it has a much greater effect upon your mind. This is why you have so much anxiety about going back to your hometown. This is the home of your unfulfilled life; but keep in mind that you are going back now with newfound purpose and meaning, because

you have transcended the life that you lived there. And because you have transcended your life there, you are free of its hold upon you; so don't worry about going back to your hometown. You are free of its karmic hold on you because you have resolved your karmic obligations there. Just go and be yourself. Your experience will inspire you to write your story We May Be Tiny, But We're Not Small. *This will be one of your best books."*

"I think I understand. Are you saying that the momentum of my regret—all of that procrastinating energy that I built up for putting off fulfilling my first life as Orest Stocco—is the cause of why I put things off today; that I am held back by the procrastinating energy of my first lifetime?"

"In effect, yes. This is why it's so hard for you to get started, even though when you do you jump in with both feet. Getting started is very hard for you, because you are held back by the memory of your unfulfilled life—"

"Is this why I have such a hard time writing my stories—because of my regret for not chasing my dream of becoming a writer in my first lifetime as Orest Stocco? Is that why it's so hard for me to begin a new story?"

"Yes. You never gave yourself to your calling to be a writer the first time you lived your life; that's why you came back to re-live it. You became a seeker this time around because you had to sever the hold that you had upon yourself; and when you found yourself you were free to become the writer that you dreamt of becoming the first time you lived your life. That's why you were inspired to write The Lion that Swallowed Hemingway. *This book was the story of how you reconciled yourself with yourself. You are free of the karmic hold that you had upon yourself because of your unfulfilled life; so forgive yourself and get on with your life of creative writing."*

"Can it be as simple as that? All I have to do is forgive myself?"

"Yes."

"Okay. Please tell me, then; how do I forgive myself? You were the Father Confessor, and you must know something about the art of forgiveness; please tell me how I can forgive myself. Let's pretend that I come to you and ask to be forgiven for my unfulfilled life; what would you say to me as the Holy Father Confessor? And I ask this with some apprehension, because I have trouble with the notion of confession; but I'd like to play this scenario out."

"It's a good exercise, and I welcome the opportunity. As Father Confessor, I read the heart of my penitents and then listened to Divine Spirit. I had the gift of understanding the sins of my penitents, and I did not judge them. I confess that it was difficult sometimes to not judge my penitents, but I was always brought back into line by Divine Spirit. I was not there to judge, but to listen and forgive and help those souls to live a better life. As I listen to your story, I am saddened by the choices you made the first time you lived your life; but my heart is filled with joy by the choices you made this time around. And I am happy to tell you that the scales have been balanced. What you did not do, you have undone; and in your undoing you found your true self. Understand that the scales of your life have been balanced, and forgiveness will be yours. Imagine a bank loan paid in full. That is how you must see your life. Go back to your hometown with the certain knowledge that you are free of its hold upon you, because you have undone all the karma that you created there; and forgiveness is a matter of understanding this. NO ONE HAS A HOLD ON YOU THERE; and the hold that you have upon yourself is all that remains. But once you forgive yourself, you will be free to live your life as a creative writer."

"What I did yesterday stays there, and I should make today a new day; is that it? Is that how I let go of the hold I have upon myself?"

*"Yes. Live your life for today, not for what you should have done yesterday or the day before. Just live your life for today and trust God. Learn to trust God. That is the biggest lesson any soul can learn. Trusting God is the heart of **the process.** There is such a deep truth to this that I have trouble expressing it; but simply by trusting God we absolve ourselves of all regrets and are free to just*

BE. This is the heart of the mystery of the self. This is why Jesus said that there is only the self and God. The self is not God, but God is the self; and you know this, because this has been your quest. Does this help you?"

"That's the heart of the mystery, isn't it? The self is not God, but God is the self; and the self is forever becoming God. Which means that God is forever becoming God through the self; is that it?"

"Yes. This is the heart of man's relationship with God. This is the mystery that all paths seek to resolve. You have resolved it, and this makes your perspective transcendent. And your stories reflect this."

"I'm sorry to ask, Padre; but can we go over once more how I can forgive myself so I can get on with my life. I know I sound like a broken record, but forgiveness does not come easily to me. I guess that's why I feel as I do about the people who have betrayed me. It's hard to forgive someone, and harder to forgive oneself. How did you forgive yourself?"

"You are right, it is very hard to forgive; especially yourself. I prayed. I prayed, and prayed, and prayed; and I begged Jesus to forgive me."

"But how did you forgive yourself? After all your prayers, you knew you had to forgive yourself; didn't you?"

"Not at first. It took me a long time to learn how to forgive myself. I learned this from my penitents. One day I realized that all the counsel that I gave to my penitents to forgive themselves for what they had done, telling them that Jesus had forgiven them—because many came back still feeling guilty for their sins—I had to apply to myself. I had to learn to forgive myself so I could counsel my penitents with an honest heart. If I could not forgive myself, how could I expect my penitents to forgive themselves? This was my secret suffering."

"Why is it so hard to forgive oneself?"

"That's a good question. Is it because we expect more of ourselves? Is it because we don't want to revisit our humiliations? Is it because we don't want to let go of our shame and hang on to

it as punishment for not doing what we should have done? I wanted to suffer for my sins. I had to learn to suffer for the joy of liberation, not for the joy of suffering. There is a difference. When you learn to suffer for the joy of liberation, you transcend your suffering and liberate yourself from the shame of your sins; and when you suffer for the sake of suffering you stay trapped in your ego. This is why Jesus said that we must die to our life to save our life. Self-forgiveness is very hard, and it may take a long time to forgive oneself. Do you remember the interview you heard yesterday of the woman who wrote Mauvais Mere (Bad Mother)? She was in her eighties and still cried for abandoning her children for a year and a half so she could go on her journey of self-discovery; her maternal guilt lasted a lifetime, and in her eighties she still had trouble forgiving herself for her selfishness. She was a young mother when she abandoned her children to go on her spiritual quest, but her call to go on her quest overrode her maternal instincts; and for this betrayal of her children she felt guilt and shame that she carried for fifty years. So it's not easy to forgive oneself, because shame goes to the core of one's being."

"Yes, I remember the interview. I was listening to it on my favorite CBC program Sunday Morning when I pulled into the parking lot at Food Basics in Midland, and rather than go into Food Basics I decided to drive to the Super Store so I could hear the rest of the interview; and I wasn't surprised to hear that she still felt shame for what she had done, because when I first heard her story a few years ago before she wrote her book I thought she was shameless in her selfishness; but apparently her shame rose to the surface, and she finally had to deal with it. That's why she wrote her memoir *Bad Mother*. She said she had to deal with her guilt, and she had trouble forgiving herself. I'm glad you reminded me, because it speaks to the issue of how difficult it is to forgive ourselves of things that have shamed us to the core."

"You may appreciate the value of Holy Confession when seen in this light, because it gives one permission to forgive oneself; but we have gone over this in your novel Healing, so we need not repeat ourselves. Suffice to say that it's all about growth and

understanding, and not about the process. Holy Confession is just another process, and in itself it is neither good nor bad (despite the karmic reality that sins are a personal responsibility that have to be redressed); and to pass judgement on the path of Holy Confession would be to miss the point of the process which is always an individual path. I won't hesitate to tell you how much joy it gave me to hear confessions. Bringing souls back to God was the greatest joy of my life, and I thank God for my mission."

"I hear the title of my nascent novel changing from *The Process* to *The Prodigal Son*. The irony is too much, given my understanding of the Way! I have to ask, is this novel possible; because suddenly it sees too far-fetched?"

"It is possible, and it is not too far-fetched. It would be a great story, regardless how clichéd the prodigal son story may be. You would be giving it a twist that would raise the message of the story to a whole new level."

"God, I'm tempted. What to do?"

"Trust God."

"You seem to be saying that a lot to me lately. Am I missing something in my dialogues with you?"

"When all is said and done, it all comes down to this: do you trust God or not? Given that you have found God, now it's up to you to trust God. Most people have not found God, as such; they either believe in God or don't, but when one finds God the dynamics of one's relationship with God changes. Take the interview you saw last night. Both Ann Baring and Andrew Harvey have found God and believe in God, and trust God enough to put themselves out there with their gnosis of God. You have been doing that with your writing also, but trusting God is always a matter of degree. My sacred contract in my lifetime as a Capuchin monk was to learn to trust God implicitly; so when I tell you to trust God, I do so because I know the way. Capisce?"

"I've been waiting a long time for you to use that word, and you couldn't have used it more appropriately! Yes, I *capisce*; and I think it's time to bring this dialogue home, because I want to go into a corner and scold myself—after I get over laughing at myself for my intransigence. Thank you, Padre."

"You're very welcome; and have a wonderful day!"

29. The Messiah Virus

Tuesday, August 26, 2014

"Good morning, Padre. Two more days to go. We're leaving for my hometown Thursday morning, and as anxious as I am I'm going to make the best of it by bringing a notebook with me. I want to capture my feelings of my return to my hometown after an eleven year absence. *God, has it been that long?* We're going to look for a realtor for our triplex. It would be so nice to sell it so we can get on with our life. I'd like to put this into your hands, Padre; so, please, see what you can do to make it happen. I would be very grateful."

"Trust God, my friend. But, yes; I will gladly see what I can do for you now that you have asked. Personal consciousness is sacrosanct and never to be interfered with; but when I am asked for help, I am obligated to assist."

"If I may ask, how can you help me? Can you manipulate time and space to bring about one's request?"

"It's more a question of alignment than manipulation. The laws of Spirit cannot be manipulated, but life can be brought into alignment with the laws of Divine Spirit; that's how miracles happen."

"I feel a hesitation this morning, and I don't have a very good connection with you. I feel like I'm forcing this dialogue, and that feels wrong."

"You have a lot on your mind because of your approaching day of departure for your hometown. The closer you get to leaving, the more compressed your feelings become; and this affects our connection. Go and make your coffee. We'll talk later..."

"I'm back. I have my coffee, and I spent a few minutes trying to find a quote from Glenda Green's book *Love without End, Jesus Speaks...* Jesus said something to Glenda that made a strong impression upon me, but I can't seem to find it. Jesus said that life is perfect, regardless of how we see it; but as I listened to Andrew Harvey online last night talking about Sacred Activism, I got the feeling that the world is on the edge of destruction, and I had trouble reconciling the two feelings—that the world is perfect and that the world is on the edge of destruction. I thought we could talk about this today."

"The Whole is always perfect, and the world is a microcosm of the Whole; so it would follow that it is perfect. But the world is an evolving planet, and it is subject to the laws of evolution; which means that every stage of the process has its own plenitude, and in itself it is always perfect but never the same as the stage before or after. These transition points of plenitude are the stages that man sees as destructive; but in themselves they are the process by which the plenitude of the next stage is made manifest. So the answer is yes and no. The world is in transition between one plenitude and another, and the process has thrown society into confusion; and it is natural for man to panic."

"Are you talking about the process of being and becoming? The process of death and rebirth? The death of one state of consciousness so another state may be born? The enantiodromiac play of life?"

"Yes. The world is in a state of change. The soul of the world has to let go of the old ways of thinking to give birth to a new way of thinking; this is what Andrew Harvey and Ann Baring are referring to."

"I don't know what to make of this. The world is going through a change like never before in the history of the planet, and I can see the chaos and confusion in world events; but as much as I would like to feel a sense of urgency to help save the planet, I'm not that way inclined. I don't know how to say this, but I'm no longer driven by the need I used to have when I first awakened to the Way and contracted the messiah virus. My fever has subsided, and I feel balanced in my spiritual perspective; but I see that Andrew Harvey is burning with the fever of the messiah virus. I love his passion and easy eloquence, but I can't help but feel that for all of his commitment to his cause of Sacred Activism, the world has its own agenda and will unfold accordingly. As modest as it may be, I feel that the most that I can do is be a good person and let the world unfold as it will."

"That is the most that anyone can do; but always bear in mind that this is your process. Andrew Harvey has his process, as does every person; so whatever one's process compels one to do that is their path to individuation. It is easy to forget that there is no one path, no one process; every soul creates its own process, and growth and understanding are inevitable. And when one has grown enough to understand that Soul is who we are, then the need to save the world will subside. Life is perfect, and there is no need to panic. Live your own process with passion, and trust God. This is the final lesson of man's journey to spiritual self-realization consciousness."

"Can we talk about the messiah virus?"

"You amuse me. Yes, of course. What would you like to say?"

"When you were the Holy Father Confessor in your earthly life, you were afflicted with the messiah virus; and by messiah virus, I mean the salvific power of the spirit of the Way, which is inherently self-transcending. When I first awakened to the Way as I lived my *Royal Dictum* (my edict of self-denial), Gurdjieff's teaching of 'work on oneself,' and the sayings of Jesus, I wanted to go out and save the world because the salvific power of the Way flowed through me like a high voltage electric current flows through a hydro line, and I don't mind telling you because I know you will understand, this threw my life into confusion because the world does not want to be saved. It took many years before I realized that the world has its own agenda, and that every person has their own relationship with God and will be saved according to their own process, and now I find it amusing when I see someone like Andrew Harvey swept away by the salvific power of the Way. And now that you are on the other side and in a state of all knowing and seeing, you must surly appreciate where I am coming from. All I'm trying to say is that I have a much deeper understanding of the Way than most people, and it amuses me to see someone who becomes afflicted with the messiah virus."

"Well put. Yes, I was afflicted with the messiah virus as I lived my own process—la via di sofferenza, if one wants to define it; and it gave me great joy to save souls from damnation. But now from my place of all knowing and seeing, I too smile at the extreme process which brought me enough growth and understanding to open the gates of Heaven; and I admire anyone whose process compels them to go out and save the world like Andrew Harvey."

"I wish I could be as accepting. Not everyone who contracts the messiah virus is worthy of my admiration like Andrew Harvey, because many so-called saviors become so inflated with Holy Spirit that they become unbalanced in their zeal to save the world, and I think they do more harm than good."

"Yes and no. The harm they do may do good that one cannot see. You had an experience with such an inflated savior when you studied that solar cult teaching, and look at how you grew in understanding—"

"At what cost?"

"Understanding doesn't come cheap. You paid a heavy price with your solar cult experience, but it was a lesson that had to be learned for your growth in understanding. Sometimes Divine Spirit puts us through sorrow to bring us the joy of liberation. All is good in the Divine Plan of God."

"GROWTH, UNDERSTANDING, and LIBERATION; that seems to be the Divine Agenda. In retrospect, all is good; but at the time of the experience, the anguish can drive one mad. I understand now that it's not about the process, as such; but one wonders if the price we pay is worth all the pain and anguish. I certainly would not repeat my life. Once was enough!"

"But you did repeat your life, my friend. This is why we are talking. We did not meet the first time you lived your life as Orest Stocco. We made arrangements for our relationship when you went back to live your life over again to change the outcome of

your life. So let me ask you now: was all the pain and anguish worth it?"

"I'd love nothing more than to say no, but I can't. Yes; it was worth it, considering that I am no longer driven by my longing to be whole. It's been one hell of a long journey from there to here, and I don't envy any person their process to their true self; but I understand now that this is the way it has to be, and there is room in my heart now for all paths and teachings."

"This is what you came back to learn. In your first lifetime as Orest Stocco, you were too set in your thinking; and you died with a lot of regret and misgivings. That's why you had to return to achieve a different outcome. And now that you have awakened to the Way, you can shine your light for others to follow. This is your destiny. So write your stories and trust God."

"I just got the feeling when you said 'trust God' that I should surrender my process to the Divine Agenda. Am I right to feel that you are asking something more of me than writing stories?"

"Andrew Harvey has his Sacred Activism, and you have your stories. Write your stories and trust God. That is all I am saying."

"The truer one is to his process, the more the Divine Agenda is made manifest; is that what you're implying?"

"Yes. No more and no less. One's process is one's path to God. Live your path with passion and trust God to do the rest."

"On that note, I thank you."

"You're welcome. But if I may be allowed a final word, you are much more of a savior than you give yourself credit for. Your writing is liberating!"

"I know; but please don't hang that label on me!"

30. The Divine Agenda

Wednesday, August 27, 2014

"Good morning, Padre. I'm frozen in stasis. We're leaving tomorrow morning for our long drive up north, and I have things to do to get ready; but I can't get motivated, like some great force is holding me back. It's my anxiety, and I don't know what to do about it; that's why I want to talk with you. I don't have anything in particular to talk about; I just need your energy to dissolve my crippling fear. May I impose upon you this morning?"

"You may. If I may, let me tell you that I enjoyed the musing that you edited this morning. It speaks beautifully to the journey of the self."

"The Pearl of Great Price?"

"Yes."

"Once I tightened it up, it made a lot more sense. I like it very much. But it is deep, and I don't know how it will go over when I post it on my blog."

"Your point will get through, regardless how deep it may be. Your readers have come to see that you think differently, and their curiosity will compel them to read your musings right through; and when they do, they will get the point that you are making, that they are their own path to growth and understanding, and this will give them a wonderful sense of relief because they won't have to feel guilty for not being more spiritual or religious."

"I'd like to ask you something about this concern that Andrew Harvey has for the world. He's driven to despair by thoughts of the world's self-immolation, but I can't seem to get worked up about this anymore. I know the world is in turmoil, especially in the Middle East; but I just don't have the same feelings that I used to have for all those people suffering. It's like my understanding of the way life unfolds has relieved me of those feelings of sorrow and pity for the suffering of humanity—not that I'm cold and callous about the suffering; I'm more indifferent than anything else. Almost like I know that this has to be because the world is being cleansed and there's not a damn thing anyone can do about it. That's why I have trouble embracing Harvey's cause of Sacred Activism. Life is an individual journey, and we are all responsible for the life we live; and I feel that as long as I live my life in the spirit of my ideal, which is to simply be a good person, I don't have to take on the karma of the world. What does that say about me?"

"That you are living your own process. This is as it should be. As I said, Andrew Harvey is living his cause of Sacred Activism because that is his process; and just because you don't resonate with his cause does not diminish the value of your process or his. Both are valid in the Divine Agenda."

"So it's all about resonance, then?"

"Essentially, yes. Which path do you resonate with? You have found your path in your own life, which is where all paths lead to; so don't feel bad because you don't have the same passion to save the world as Andrew Harvey or any other savior. Saving the world is a wonderful cause, if one's process calls for one to save the world. The Divine Agenda has room for everyone's process, and that's all one needs to know to relieve oneself of any guilt for not feeling more concerned about the world."

"And if I may ask, is the world headed for destruction?"

"There will be a lot of suffering yet to come, but not destruction in the sense of an apocalypse. The world will avoid that catastrophe."

"Padre, I had a revelation with my last spiritual musings, "A Cricket in My Window," and I'd like to run it by you. My musing led me to see that there is nothing special about me being a writer; or, as I expressed it in my musing, *'So, I'm a writer? Big deal!'* But this feeling of being just another person has had a profound effect upon my psyche, and I feel rather stupid now because I could have spent my energies much more productively and provided Penny and myself a much more economically stable retirement. As it is, we still have a way to go for the kind of life that would have been easily realized had I not spent so much time and energy seeking and writing; but I know what you're going to say. You're going to say that was my process; right?"

"No. That was your calling. You had to heed your calling or you would never have achieved the outcome that you came back to realize. Yours is a special life, because you came back to live it over again; and few souls have wisdom and courage to re-live the same life over again with the intention of achieving a different outcome. This was your calling, and given what you achieved you have no need to berate yourself for not having a more stable economic life. That will come, and you and your loved one will have the life you want to live. Trust God. That's the final answer."

"So this was written in the Divine Agenda?"

"It was written, but you were the author. Every soul is free to choose the life it lives, and the Divine Agenda gives us the freedom to live it."

"I'm a little confused. Is the Divine Agenda a master plan, or an open-ended program that allows for editorial changes; like a play in the theater that goes through all kinds of rehearsals and rewrites before we get to see the finished product?"

"That's a very good analogy. Life is very much like a play, and we have to rehearse and rewrite our script many times before we get it right. Yes; the Divine Agenda is an open-ended program. God does give us the freedom to play out whatever choice we make. This is the beauty of man's relationship with God. Your life is living proof of the re-written script. You came back to your same life because you felt you did not get it right the first time; but this time you feel much more resolved and fulfilled. You chose a different process this time around, and you achieved a different outcome. As I said, there is room in the Divine Agenda for every process, and every process is guided by Divine Spirit; that's what connects the individual process with the Divine Agenda. We are never separate from God who gave us life and the freedom to live it as we choose."

"So the Divine Agenda's imperative is to see to it that every soul is free to realize its spiritual destiny?"

"Yes. To become our Divine Self."

"Through our own process?"

"There is no other way. Each person's life is their path to their Divine Self, because their Divine Self is the realization of their own individuation process, just as you realized in your spiritual musing 'The Pearl of Great Price.'"

"Okay, I think I got it. Now I have to face the music and get off my ass and do what I have to do today. God, I hate myself for putting off what I should have taken care of years ago! I just hate myself!"

"As a young Confessor, I found that sins of omission were the most difficult sins to forgive, but I found it in my heart to forgive them also; and in time, sins of omission proved to be the most treasured gift of all, because it gave the penitent the wisdom to plan their life with much more care and attention. You have failed to take care of all your responsibilities as a landlord, and now you suffer the anxiety of your sins of omission; but no one was hurt. No one suffered. You're not going to go to Hell for not being a more responsible landlord. As you said in your spiritual musing about being a writer, what's the big deal? It's all in your head, my dear friend. Stop worrying about it."

"Thank you for that. My Demon Fear got hold of me and won't let go; so I guess I have no choice but stand up to him and tell him to go back where he came from; but where is that, if I may ask?"

"Didn't we have this discussion? Didn't we say that fear is ego-driven? Let go of your attachment to your guilt for not being a more responsible landlord and better provider for Penny and your Demon Fear will have no more power over you. Guilt is the energy that gives life to your Demon Fear. Forgive yourself, my friend. Forgiveness is the great healer. Don't be so hard on yourself. You are not a bad provider. Count all of your blessings. You have a beautiful home in Georgian Bay that is mortgage free, you have tenants for your triplex, and life is not so hard even with your

heart condition; so why must you suffer the guilt of not doing more than what you have? Forgive yourself for what you could have done but didn't, and get on with your life. Try it. Take a moment and repeat after me: I FORGIVE MYSELF FOR NOT BEING A MORE RESPONSIBLE LANDLORD. I FORIGVE MYSELF FOR NOT BEING A BETTER PROVIDER. I FORGIVE MYSELF FOR PUTTING THINGS OFF. AND I FORGIVE MYSELF FOR ALL MY SINS OF OMISSION, BECAUSE GOD FORGIVES ME. Now go and do what you have to do for your trip up north; and keep in mind that I am with you every moment of the day. God bless you, my beloved friend."

"Thank you, Padre. I needed that!"

31. Today's the Day

Thursday, August 28, 2014

"Good morning, Padre; though I don't feel like greeting you this morning because I'm not in the best of spirits. It's my fault, and I don't really want to go there. It's that tight-rope thing you talked about in one of my spiritual healing sessions with you, but that's a metaphor I don't want to explain right now. Suffice to say that I would like to forgive myself for falling off the tightrope and start my day fresh with new hopes; though I don't know how it's going to unfold seeing that we are going to be leaving in a few hours to drive up north, which still fills me with anxiety. I repeated what you asked me to say yesterday, forgiving myself, and I did feel a little better; but I don't think I got to the core of my being with my forgiveness. So, being the Holy Father Confessor for most of your life on earth, may I ask how you learned how to forgive; because as easy as it appears to be, I think it's one of the hardest things in the world to do? Can we talk about forgiveness today?"

"Good morning, my friend. Please don't feel embarrassed. I am aware of everything you do, and why you do it; and it is because we do not know why people do the things they do that it is so difficult to forgive. This was my biggest challenge, and it took many years before I learned how to forgive with an open heart. At first I had to trust Jesus and our Holy Father to do the forgiving, but as I learned to read the hearts of my penitents I began to understand the power of sin; and this opened up my heart to more of God's love, and forgiveness became easier. God's love for us is infinite in its mercy, and there is nothing that we can do that will stop God from loving us; this is how I learned to forgive with an open heart, because of God's infinite mercy."

"Forgiveness is about acceptance, then? I have to accept what has taken place and not judge it; is that how I learn to forgive?"

"It is difficult to not judge, because we are all brought up with some kind of moral values; and learning how to accept what one has done without judging them with our moral standards can be very hard to do because it offends our sense of right and wrong. But right or wrong, what is done is done; and today's another day. Accept the past for what it is, and let it go; that's the first step in forgiving with an open heart. What can you do about yesterday?"

"Are you asking me?"

"Yes."

"Nothing. What's done is done. All I have is the memory."

"And what good does it do you to cling to a memory that reminds you of what you should have done?"

"Nothing."

"Then forgive yourself and enjoy your day."

"Okay. Thank you, and until the next time..."

32. Back into the Lion's Den

Wednesday, September 10, 2014

"Good morning, Padre. I don't know where to begin. Penny and I came back from our trip up north on Sunday. We left Thunder Bay Saturday morning, after we delivered the eviction notice in person to our tenant who avoided us all day Friday, and on our drive to Nipigon I got stopped by the OPP and got a fine for three hundred and twenty dollars for not having my license renewed. I did not even know it had expired on my birthday in July, so that put another damper on our trip; but had I not been stopped who knows how long I would be driving with an expired licence? We stopped at Bruce Mines for dinner at Bobber's and we stayed at the Bavarian Motel for the night and pulled into our yard late in the afternoon. All in all, our trip to my hometown of Nipigon gave me enough material to finish the book that I could not write until I did return to the lion's den. Well, Padre; I have to tell you, I got the shock of my life when I stepped back into the lion's den, because the den was empty. The lion had long since died of dementia, and I was living in false fear for years. I don't know what to make of my whole experience. I'm, going to explore it for my new book *We May Be Tiny, But We're Not Small.* We have to go back up north in the first week of October to paint the apartment that is going to be vacated, and I hope there will be no trouble with the tenant who caused us enough aggravation as it is. What do you think of our whole situation? Wasn't it something, I had to go and kick the devil out of our house in person? The liar and cheat and trickster played me for a fool, and I've come back to Georgian Bay a chastened man."

"Our most valuable lessons are hard come by, but they prove to be invaluable to our growth. Good morning, my good friend. You did have a very eventful trip, and much more rewarding than you realize. The dynamics of your life have been changed because

of this trip. Now you can take charge of your life, which you could not do until you dealt with your issues from your hometown. But now that you know the lion is dead, you are free to get on with your life; and please write your book. Tell the whole story. Don't hold anything back. This is going to be the big book of your life. I am very proud of you and Penny. You are on the road to the best years of your life. I promise you."

"Okay, I have to ask you some hard questions now. What did I step into up north? What was all that nonsense going on in my house? Why did the devil take up residence in my beautiful apartment?"

"The play of opposites is always at work in life, and the good that you and Penny created was eventually taken over by the bad in people; but the change back to the good has begun, so do not worry."

"And about my hometown. I feel like I stepped into a time warp. I can't quite explain how I feel about my experience there. The downtown has changed. I don't recognize it. All of my attachment to my hometown has vanished. I feel like the town has no more hold on me, and this I feel to be a healing experience. But I did have a rude awakening for this healing!"

"You certainly did. But you needed to be awakened from your emotional attachment to your hometown. Your attachment kept you in fear. But as you so humorously put it, when you stepped back into the lion's den the lion wasn't there. It had long since died—"

"Of dementia!"

"Very well put. And that should be the first line of your new novel."

"Okay. This will be the first line of my new novel *We May Be Tiny, But We're Not Small*: 'I went back into the lion's den, but the den was empty; the lion had long since died of dementia...'"

"Start your book this winter, when you have settled into your writing comfort. It will come on its own, and it will be worthy of your effort."

"About our house. We're putting it up for sale. We're going to be going back up north in the spring to do some outside work to spruce up the house, and I hope we get a buyer. Can I put this in your capable hands?"

"By all means. Do what you have to do and trust God. You're in God's hands, and all will go according to your dreams and wishes. I promise you."

"I have to thank you for your support, Padre. I cannot begin to explain the fear and anxiety and apprehension that I had of stepping back into the lion's den; but it was all in my head! Wow! What a rude awakening I got! It's going to make great material for my novel, though!"

"That's how great novels are made. I'm happy for your outcome. And it will only get better from here."

"I have to tell you that I haven't slept with the radio on ever since our trip up north, and I am finally getting some sleep that is refreshing. I hope I can get back to a regular sleeping pattern so I can get my life back."

"You will. It's all happening now. You have shed the guilt that held you back and are free to let your mind relax."

"This was a trip in learning to accept my responsibilities, wasn't it?"

"Yes."

"And this takes a lot of pressure off Penny, doesn't it?"

"Which she well deserves."

"I know. And I have to make it up to her somehow. I hope I can."

"Just share in her concern for you and you will make her happy."

"I have to ask you, did I step back into my old parallel life; or was this trip back to Nipigon an entirely new parallel world?"

"You stepped back into the parallel world that was created after you left Nipigon. Your departure caused a shift in consciousness in that community, and its reality got altered. The town you left is not the same town. Your books caused a dramatic shift in the consciousness of that town, and it was forced to wake

up to its shadow side; and this caused a change in its reality. The town you stepped into this time is the new Nipigon after the change that you affected by leaving the community. The town will never know this, though. You feel different because you are different. The people recognize you, but don't know you. They don't know what to make of you. You are too much for them."

"I'm back to my old theme: people don't want to know themselves. They are afraid of what they might find. I learned this from an old friend that I knew for over forty years. We spent Saturday afternoon together. He's a lot older now, but basically the same man—a skeptic who can't step out of his own mind to see the world with fresh eyes. He saddened me, Padre."

"His journey is one of learning, your journey is one of discovery; the two don't go well together, because what you have discovered throws his world into confusion. You shook up his world with your books. He doesn't know what to make of you now. He's totally confused about you."

"I can understand that. I'm confused about me myself. This has been one remarkable experience, and I can't wait to explore it in my new novel. Okay, Padre; thank you for our little chat. Until the next time..."

33. The Screen of Life

Saturday, September 13, 2014

"Good morning, Padre. I'd like to run an idea by you about a new novel that I've been nudged to write; a novel that would be a take-off from my novel *The Golden Seed*. My character Peter Augustino drops his Roman Catholic faith for reasons that are explained in the novel, but after many years of seeking and finding the answers he was looking for he is inspired to return to his Christian faith, but with an enlightened understanding of Christ's teaching which makes his return to the Church an entirely novel experience because he would be embracing his Christian faith on enlightened terms now. What do you think of this idea for a novel? My working title would be "The Prodigal Son." Peter would be the son that left the Church but returns on his terms."

"I think this is an excellent idea. This concept would be novel indeed, and it would throw a lot of light on the original teachings of Jesus. I would suggest you outline your story and work it out in plot form, as you once did with some of your other stories. Draw your circle and let each spoke of the circle be a chapter, and work it from there. This way you can give the story the depth and passion of your own journey, but in an entirely fictional context. Your working title is excellent. It will get you where you need to go."

"Am I going to live long enough to write this book, and the other books that I want to write?"

"Yes. Your sacred contract is for you to write all the books that you intend to write. It will happen. Trust God."

"Okay. Now I want to share something with you. Ever since we came back from up north I feel different about life. I feel like the prisoner who escaped from Plato's cave and I see life now as a projection on the walls of the cave; to be more contemporary, it feels to me that life is a projection upon the screen of life, and illusory. It's just a Soul projection, and no more; and I get the distinct feeling that every person's life is their soul's projection on the screen of life, and they have to play it out as they project it. This makes life a very singular experience, although within the context of the world play, if I may be allowed to express it this way. Do you understand what I'm trying to say? I just feel that I'm outside the illusion of the play of life, and I feel very much alone and almost foolish in my sacred knowledge."

"This mystery takes many lifetimes to resolve. You have come to that point in your life where the inner workings of the universe are being revealed to you. Yes, every person's life is a projection on the Big Screen of the Mind; and every person's life is their own within the context of the world play. You are correct to believe that there is only one reality, but how we experience that reality depends upon our individual state of consciousness. The parallel worlds do exist, but they are states of consciousness. But because Consciousness is one, there really are no parallel worlds. It's all a state of Mind."

"And our purpose in life, is?"

"To grow in understanding. This is how God experiences God. We exist because God loves us and wants us to participate in the experience of God. Soul is God's vehicle to God, and we are seeds that come into the world to grow and blossom in God Consciousness. It's that simple."

"So it's all real and not real at one and the same time?"

"In one sense, yes; but in another sense, no. Life is life, and it has its own course to follow. The laws of life govern life's growth, but soul has the freedom to grow beyond where life can take it. This is God's gift to man."

"Padre, I've been re-reading one of the biographies of your life, *Padre Pio, Man of Hope,* by Renzo Allegri, and I'm excited by the details of your sacred life; but I'd like to know if you were spiritually awakened when you spoke from the consciousness of all-knowing, or were these moments of spontaneous omniscience?"

"At the time, they were spontaneous; and they puzzled me as much as they puzzled others. But over time I became more and more awakened spiritually, and I spoke from a consciousness of all knowing and seeing."

"But it didn't manifest entirely until you crossed over to the other side, when you became one with Divine Spirit?"

"Yes. Once I crossed over I was free to be Soul."

"I don't know where this is going, Padre; but I feel that my journey of self-discovery has entered a new phase, and I attribute this to my trip up north where I learned that the lion had died of dementia!"

"This is true. Your fear kept you from further discovery. Now you are on your way to the deeper mysteries of life."

"Here's something else that I learned since my return from up north: I feel that people don't care about the meaning and purpose of life. People are too caught up in their own survival— be it the good life or just a life—to really care; and I feel that all of my writing is like dust blowing in the wind. By this I mean that all the thought and reflection that I have put into understanding the meaning and purpose of life won't mean a damn thing to anyone but myself; and this makes me feel sad, because I know how useful this knowledge could be for those that do have a longing to know."

"You never know what's in a person's heart. Every person has their own relationship with God, and in their own way they care; but it doesn't show on the outside, because people don't want to show this side of their life. You have taken the liberty to share your thoughts and reflections, and they are and will be much appreciated; so don't worry about it. Your writing is for you, but it is also for the world. This is the way it's meant to be. Even this book of dialogues will find its place in the library of the Way, and people will appreciate how you opened yourself up the way you do. As I keep telling you, trust God."

"By trusting God, you mean I should just do what I feel I should do and let God take care of the rest?"

"Yes."

"I've been reading *Healing with Padre Pio* just to get that wonderful feeling of being with you, and I'm sorry if this sounds immodest, but damn that novel reads well! Will it ever find its audience?"

"Yes, it does read well; and yes, it will find its audience. The day is not far off. Once you make the break into the marketplace, your books will find their readers. This is written in the Big Screen of your life. Trust God."

"That's all for today, Padre. My computer keys are giving me a problem. I got the problem corrected, but I want to break off for now. Until the next time, I remain your faithful companion."

34. Request for Intercession

Tuesday, September 16, 2014

"Good morning, Padre. It seems that my tenant wants to give me a problem. He got his eviction notice when we went up north, but he wants to be recalcitrant; and I would ask that you intercede and have him gracefully vacate our apartment so Penny and I can get on with the sale of the house and our life. Would you please intercede for us?"

"I will do everything I can to help you get on with your life. Your tenant has his problems, and I put him in God's hands."

"I don't want to be merciless, but we gave that young man every opportunity to get his life on track; but he betrayed our trust. What else could we do but evict him?"

"You did what you had to do. Now let me do what I have to do. Do not worry about him. His life is in God's hands, and he will be moved out by the end of the month without any trouble. I promise you."

"Why have I been such a fool? Can you please tell me?"

"You trust too much. You have always trusted too much. Your belief in human nature has often been the cause of much of your suffering, but that is not a bad thing; because of your trust, you found God."

"Can I be assured that we won't have any problems with my tenant? We don't need that anxiety at this time in our life. My heart can't take the stress. What else can I do?"

"Get plenty of rest. And go for walks. You need to do more walking, or biking, or both. This will strengthen your heart muscle."

"And I've lost my inspiration for writing. I won't be able to really get back into it until we put our triplex up for sale. Again I ask, will you intercede for us and help sell our triplex? This will ease our anxiety considerably."

"This has already been set into motion. Just do what you have to do and let God and me take care of the rest."

"God, I'm becoming a wimp! What's happening to me?"

"Nothing out of the ordinary. Just age. As you grow older, you take stock of your life; and you have yet to accomplish your goal of being acknowledged as a writer. That is coming soon. Trust me, my friend; this is all in the cards that you have dealt yourself. They have to be seen by the world, because it has been deemed by Providence. Your point of view is valued by everyone who cares about the soul of man, and your work will be read by many—and before you die. I promise this upon my mother's love."

"Padre, I don't mean to have you assure me with your mother's love, which was as sacred to you as Christ's love. Please pardon me."

"No need to be pardoned. You are who you are, and I am who I am; and, truth be told, we are very much alike."

"I'd love to visit San Giovanni Rotonda. I'd love to take Penny there and have her experience Italy, the town where you were born and the monastery where you spent most of your life. I'd love that, Padre. Please, if you could help make that happen I would be so grateful!"

"It will be the best holiday of your entire life. You and your loved one will enjoy yourselves as never before. I promise you this holiday."

"I would like to know, after all that you experienced in your life, did you really still have doubts at the end? I can't believe what I read."

"My doubts were real, but only because I refused to let go of the hold they had upon me. But you are right. I was on firm ground when I passed over, and my doubts had no more power over me."

"I hesitate to say this, but why does the world continue to be so resistant to the reality of the spiritual life? Your life proved to the world that God is not a figment of our imagination; and yet the world persists. Am I just making an argument for the sake of talking?"

"*No. It is a real concern for you. You have crossed over to the side of the all-knowing, and you cannot fathom how the world can be so dense. But consider how long it took you to get here? Such is the way of life. Do not concern yourself about the world and its way to all-knowing. Life is a journey of the self, and the self is not the collective. The collective marches to its own tune, and it has its own destiny. This is the reality of the world.*"

"Will I ever be anxiety free? Free enough to enjoy my life with Penny the way I have dreamt? I do so much want to see her happy."

"*As I said, trust God. You are in good hands. You will see your dream come true. You are in fact living your dream, and I adore you both.*"

"And I adore and love and respect and admire and appreciate you like you were my father and brother and closest friend. Thank you, Padre."

"*You're welcome, my dear friend.*"

"I so hope that we can work together on another book. I do so hope we can do this next summer. I keep reading *Healing with Padre Pio* just to get the feel of your presence, because even though I know you are here in these dialogues it does not feel the same as when you came through the medium who channeled you. Is this book going to be written?"

"*Yes. And it will surprise you. It will begin as you planned, but it will find its own way, as all of your books do. I cannot wait to work with you again on another book. This exercise that we are doing now is preparation for the book to come. This will serve you in good stead.*"

"I think I have covered what I had to say. I thank you for your time and patience and love and understanding. It helps me considerably."

"*I am always with you, my dear and good friend. Ciao for now.*"

"*Ciao, Padre...*"

35. Request Granted

Saturday, September 20, 2014

"Thank you, Padre. We got an email from our obstreperous tenant informing us that he will be out of the apartment by the end of this month, and that he will clean it and leave the keys with one of our other tenants. I don't know how you did it, but this relieves us of a lot of anxiety and will make our trip up north at the end of this month much more enjoyable."

"You're more than welcome. And you are right, you and Penny will enjoy your trip up north this time. It will be anxiety free. And you will enjoy working on your apartment. It will be a special time for both of you. And the apartment will look lovely and help to sell your triplex."

"Thank you for that. I have to learn to trust God more, don't I?"

"It's not that you don't trust God so much as you letting your worries get the best of you. I learned over the course of my life just how burdensome life can be for people, but in the end all of man's worries are for naught. That's why my motto was, 'pray, hope, and don't worry.' I tried to console my penitents by giving them hope. That's all I'm doing with you. And the best way to give one hope is to get them to trust God. In God, all hopes come true."

"That's what I tried to do with my niece this morning in my email to her in which I shared a dream that Penny had that spoke to her current life situation. My niece has just had a cancer scare. She is waiting for more test results, and her life has been thrown into confusion. On the phone the other day I felt compelled to tell her to read my two books, *Healing with Padre Pio* and *The Golden Seed;* and Penny's dream the other night was a message confirming that my niece read these two books. I explained the reason why in my email this morning as I interpreted Penny's dream. Did I interpret her dream correctly?"

"It was more than ample. Your niece will appreciate Penny's dream and your interpretation, and she will read your two books and get what she needs to help her in her time of need. I am watching over her. She has been in my care from the day of her birth. Her family is in my prayers all the time."

"Padre, is my life finally coming around? Are things really going to go as smoothly as Penny and I would like? I feel we're on a new wave about to roll into the great ocean of peace and joy. Am I dreaming?"

"No. It is a new wave, as you say; and you are on your way to the life that you and your loved one have always wanted. The tide has turned for you, and I am happy that you can finally see it happening. It's been happening for a long time now, but you couldn't see it. Now you can, and this makes me happy."

"Well, it's been a long time coming. I can only hope that this new wave can carry us all the way to the end with joy and happiness. As I once told you in one of my spiritual healing sessions, I would love to go out of this life with the blessed virtues of quiet dignity and sweet humility. I hope I do."

"A noble ambition. I too wished for these virtues. But as you realized, one must assume the virtues to have them—"

"Alright, I get the point! You're a wonderful companion, Padre. I'd like so much to share in your company in person. It's fun in spirit, but it would be so much more rewarding face to face. Maybe someday."

"Make the most of your day, my good friend. We will enjoy each other's company one day, face to face. We have much work to do before we do, though; so just keep on doing what you are doing. And trust God."

"Yeah, I know! Okay, that's all for today..."

36. Going back into the Lion's Den

Monday, September 29, 2014

"Good morning, Padre. Penny and I are going up north again, to my hometown, and we're hoping that our tenant will be moved out of the top apartment of our triplex so we can paint it and get our triplex ready to put on the market. We want to sell it because it would make our life a lot easier; so, Padre, we could use your help. In any event, I don't know what books I should bring to read in the mornings with my coffee while we're staying at Penny's sister's house. I've chosen *PHILOSOPHY: 100 Essential Thinkers*, and *The Three "Only Things"*, by Robert Moss. And I'm bringing my notebook. I hope we have a safe and productive trip with no surprises."

"You will have a safe and productive trip. Your life is on a different trajectory now. You have come to that point in your growth and understanding where you will contribute to life in a different way. You began with your conversation with your friends over and after dinner on Saturday. You made a very strong impression, and this is only the beginning of the path of your new trajectory. I promise you that all is going to unfold according to your dreams."

"I've initiated this exercise in active imagination with you this morning because I need your support. I feel a little uneasy about going back to my hometown again, though certainly not as uneasy as I did a few weeks ago when we went up; that proved to be quite an experience. I hope you don't mind me addressing you. I do feel such comfort in my dialogues with you, despite the nature of the exercise."

"The exercise does not matter. What matters is the outcome. If it makes you feel better, we will have accomplished our task."

"I have to ask you something. My friend Alice, who came for dinner at our place on Saturday with her friend Martha, woke up one morning with your name on her lips. She repeated your name twice, and she knew she had to come and see me; and then a coincidence occurred to help make up her mind: she was going to call her friend to invite her to come and visit Penny and me, but her friend called her instead and invited Alice to go with her on a one day retreat in Wyevale, just five minutes from our home; and Alice saw this as the sign she needed to come and visit me, especially since she had some questions to ask me about my novel *Healing with Padre Pio*. So, is she ready now to step onto a new path in her healing journey?"

"She is, and she has taken the first step by visiting you and Penny. She wanted to be sure that you and Penny were still on the same path as her, and it gave her much comfort to know that you have not left the path that has become her life; but she needed more than that from you. She needed the energy, and she got what she needed to assist her on her healing journey."

"A change in attitude?"

"Yes. She had to change her focus. Your novel Healing with Padre Pio gave her the shift she needed to see herself with fresh eyes. Now she can focus on herself in a different way. She can love herself more freely and the healing energy can flow with less obstruction into her life."

"I don't want to ask if her cancer will be healed because that is between her and God, but I do hope the very best for her Padre. I like her. She is a good person trying her very best. Please, if it is not a violation of any spiritual law, I ask for your help for her. Can I do that?"

"Of course you can. She has opened up to this avenue of assistance, and she has already made the request on the inner. I am with her as we speak."

"Padre, will people ever care? What am I experiencing now? I feel like I'm on a completely different track. What's going on with me?"

"As I said, you are on a new trajectory. Your path has changed insomuch that you are more in the trenches of life, but with an enlightened awareness of the purpose of life. This makes the same

experience of life different. As you said when you quoted the Buddhist saying, 'Before enlightenment, you chop wood and carry water. After enlightenment, you chop wood and carry water.' This is you now after enlightenment, and it feels strange to you; but you will adjust to your new reality, and all will be much better than you can hope for."

"And my writing. Will I get my inspiration back?"

"It's never gone away. You will write with a shift in your perspective. This will make your writing more accessible. You have much to write yet."

"Is it worth the bother, that's what I'm asking?"

"Don't write for the world, as such; write for your own edification. In your writing, you grow in understanding. Write with love, and your love will find its place in the world. I promise you."

"You've reached out to two people that I know of with my novel *Healing with Padre Pio*—my niece, who is going through a cancer scare, and my friend Alice who is in throes of a cancer-healing journey—and I wonder if this isn't the advent of many more to come?"

"It is. Your novel is just beginning to make an impact on the consciousness of the world. It will continue and it will reach many people. You have given me an entry into the world that I hoped your novel would. Thank you."

"You're thanking me. Writing that novel was the best thing I ever did. It saved me from myself!"

"Yes. And now it can help save others from themselves. That was the point of writing that novel. That's what we agreed to do long before you came back into the world. Yes, you have accomplished your goals in life; and now you are free to live the rest of your life as you dreamt of doing. I promise you."

"We will be leaving around nine o'clock this morning, and I ask for you guidance and protection on our whole journey and experience when I step back into the lion's den. I know that the lion is dead, and that it died of dementia as I like to say; but I still have emotional issues that I have to resolve there, and I need all the comfort and support that I can get. I hope I don't sound like a wimp, but life has been a real struggle for me in my efforts to achieve a different outcome with my parallel life; so please forgive me if I'm not as strong as I would like to be. It has been a lonely journey. But thanks to Penny, we are here safe and sound. Wounded, but safe and sound."

"No need to apologize. You should be proud of yourself. Both of you. You do me proud. And, believe me when I say this, but I look forward to our next book together. It will happen next summer. That I can promise you for sure!"

"Thank you. I needed that confirmation. And our economic reality?"

"Sound. Don't worry. The cards are in play. You have a winning hand, and your timing is in sync with life. Just do what you have to do and let God take care of the rest. You are in good hands."

"I want to trust God. That's what the whole journey is about, isn't it?"

"Yes and no. The acorn has to become an oak tree first; but it helps to learn to trust God along the way. That's what the journey is all about."

"Okay. Until we return from up north..."

37. Life Is a Bag of Tricks

"Why, I'm not entirely sure; but I think it's because I wasn't ready yet to talk with you about my trip up north. What a difference two weeks makes. We went up north full of doubt and anxiety, and we came home resolved—but only because our tenant had vacated the apartment and left a pig sty for us to clean. But I can come back to this another time. For now I want to just say hello and thank you for your guidance, because I know you had a hand in how everything unfolded; so, thank you Padre for looking after us—"

"*You're welcome. And what did you learn from this experience?*"

"Enough to write my book now. I could not write my novel *We May Be Tiny, But We're Not Small* until I returned to the lion's den; and now I can sit down and write it. If I had to sum up what I leaned, it would be this: life is a bag of tricks. I came back from the lion's den resolved of all my anxieties about our triplex and my feelings about my hometown, which were a tangled web of imagined horrors; and I am so thankful for your comforting words. They helped me through my whole experience. I can't talk about it now, but you know what I'm referring to."

"*I do. This is the material you need to write your next novel, which you will begin when the snow flies—as you are wont to do every year to begin your creative process; and you will pour yourself into this novel as never before.*"

"I have something that I want to say, or ask you, which has not yet risen to the surface of my mind; but I can feel it rising, and I want to get it out. It has to do with my new feelings about life. My re-entry into the lion's den has changed my life. I no longer feel as I used to. I feel remarkably different; but I cannot put this into words yet. Perhaps this is what's going to drive my new novel. I can try to explain how I feel, but I don't know if I can. I just know that life no longer seems to me what it used to seem. It seems to me like one big mirage now, but a mirage of such realism that it has usurped all of my old images of life; like I have been touched by such a devastating dose of reality that everything people do and say has taken on a completely new meaning for me, as though they are walking through life asleep to what life is all about, and I feel like the only one awake!"

"You did have a rude awakening. Perhaps this is what it means to have a rude awakening. You experienced the reality that disposed your imagined reality."

"But what of everyone else? Are they asleep to life?"

"Yes. This is how it's meant to be. Sleepwalking through life is the normal way for those that are not ready to take up the secret way. You have taken up the secret way and with each step you wake up a little more. Your foray back into the lion's den has shocked you into the stark reality of human nature—that not everyone is to be trusted. This is a lesson that you HAD to learn. You simply trust too much, and you pay for it every time. This time you paid in spades."

"I did. But I'm proud of the way I handled it. I tried with all my might to keep an even keel, and we saw the experience right to the end. It cost Penny and me a great deal, but we did pull it off. Now we can get on with selling the triplex."

"It was necessary to get the house in order and your emotions cleared up, because you could not continue with your life until you did. Now you can go on and write the story that has been waiting to be written, the sequel to What Would I Say Today If I Were to Die Tomorrow? I look forward to reading it."

"I'd really like to finish writing *Enantiodromia and Other Stories* first. I feel obliged to complete this book of short stories."

"You will. Just go with your instincts. You are in a better position now to just let it flow without all that emotional baggage to drag you down."

"Padre, would you mind if I interrupt this dialogue? I'm being called to go outside and do some leafing. We can take this up later, or tomorrow morning, if you don't mind—"

"Not at all. The fresh air will do you good..."

"I did do my leafing yesterday, and then my neighbor Tony came over shortly after lunch to borrow our lawn tractor. It wouldn't start, so we had to give the battery a boost with my van; and then Tony cut his lawn. He had blown his leaves yesterday morning also and wanted to cut his lawn for the last time this fall, and while he was cutting his lawn I raked the pile of leaves that I had on my front lawn and discarded them in the empty lot next to ours where they will break down and decompose. It's nice to have a couple of empty lots beside our house. In any event, after Tony did his lawn I cut our front lawn as well; and today I am going to blow the leaves in our back yard and then cut the lawn for the last time this year. I hope I can get the lawn tractor started. I think I will have to boost the battery again.

"On to another subject. This morning I continued reading Jung's *Memories, Dreams, Reflections* (I've read it three times already and dipped into it many times), and then I picked up his tome *Mysterium Coniunctionis*, which brought his life's work to conclusion, and I don't mind telling you Padre, but it scared the shit out of me because it is so unbelievably ponderous. I'm not capable of understanding it, and I don't want to make the effort to do so; and I feel guilty for not trying. And then I thought to myself, that was his path; that was his way, and it took him deep into the study of Gnosticism and alchemy, and that was not my way as such. My way was by way of Gurdjieff and the way of life, and I achieved what I came into this world to achieve—to find my lost soul. And here I am. Now what?"

"Now you live your life. You write about your life. That is your way. You are right to say that that was Jung's way. As I said, life is a journey of the self; and no two selves are the same. The hardest thing for one to do is to live their own life. You are ahead of the

game because you realize that life is an individual journey, so don't fret over what you cannot understand. Life is too big to understand it all. Pick one little corner of life and try to make sense of it, and the rest will reveal itself to you according to your need. That's how life works."

"Okay. Thanks. Now on to the question of my creative spirit. I want to reconnect with it. I've lost touch—not completely, but enough to scare me—and I have to reconnect, because that's the only thing that gives me complete satisfaction. I don't have the worry of our triplex at the back of my mind haunting me now, and I hope to get back into my writing care-free, so to speak; how can I reconnect with my creative spirit and get back into the flow of creative writing?"

"Write, write, and write; that's how. You know that to do you must do. That's the law of life. Doing is the entry point to all tasks. Just pick something and write. That's your entry point that will connect you with your creative spirit."

"I knew that, but fear has kept be from jumping in."

"Fear keeps everyone from doing. Fear is man's mortal enemy, but it can also be a great motivator. Challenge yourself to write the story you fear the most. Start with other stories first, and then when you feel strong enough challenge yourself to write the story you fear writing the most. That will be your most personal story, and it might just be your best—because it will be the story that most speaks your way."

"I think I understand that. In a dream one night I saw a man in his fifties tell a younger man who was his friend that he wanted him to meet me. The young man wanted to know why his older friend wanted him to meet me, and the older man said to his young friend, **'Because he knows.'** In my dream this man felt that I was a man who knew the secret of life, and he wanted his young friend to meet me; and you know what, Padre, I do feel that I am a knower of life, if I may use that phrase. I may not understand life in all of its complexity, but I know the purpose of life—which is to become our true self. Is this what the man in my dream meant?"

"Yes. You are a knower of life. That is a good way of putting it. You found the Way, and you lived the Way, and in living the Way the secret of life revealed itself to you—just as it did to your mentor Carl Gustav Jung who found the secret of life through his studies of the ancient teachings. A knower of life knows the secret of life, and it is your duty now to reveal it to the world through your own discovery, which means through your writing. This way the secret is passed on to those who are ready to receive it. This is your mission for the rest of your life."

"And I can't help but feel that this is to be done through creative fiction; or, to be more precise, autobiographical fiction—just as Thomas Wolfe, whom I just discovered, did with his writing. There's a parallel between his creative impulse and mind. He's the author who said, 'You can't go home again.' Which I'm going to use for my novel *We May Be Tiny, But We're Not Small.*"

"That is what you have been called to do for the rest of your life, and the sooner you get at it the better."

"I get it. I am a procrastinator, aren't I? That's always been my problem. I put things off, and off, and off and then they catch up to me—like putting off going up north to tend to our triplex. It caught up to me and came crashing down on me and I had to deal with it. God, what an experience! Thank you for your help, Padre."

"I was happy to be of assistance. So, what's on your agenda today?"

"I'm going to do some more leafing and hopefully cut the rest of the lawn and then I'm going to get dinner ready. I think I'm going to put on a spaghetti sauce, with spareribs. Thursday is often our pasta day. Penny loves spaghetti. Which reminds me of the time your friend the good Doctor got a lady to cook you a plate of *spaghetti ala napoletana,* which you appreciated very much but which you asked your good friend to give it to one of the poor peasants who could use it more than you. I'll never forget that little sacrifice you made. It spoke your whole character!"

"Thank you for reminding me. Yes, he was a good man, my friend; but we see each other quite regularly here on the other side. Life goes on, my friend; and the friends you make are forever."

"I believe that, because there is a special bond that comes with friendship that can't be spelled out. It goes to the core of one's soul."

"That is how you have affected your neighbor Tony. He feels that special connection and loves you very much."

"Yes, I know; and you know what, Padre. The other day when I went over to visit him he was so happy to see me that he gave me a big hug. He thought something had happened to me and was worried. He came over to our house when Penny and I were up north and he was so worried that he went to one of our neighbors to ask about me. The lady told him she thought we were up north, and this relieved his fear of something having happened to me (he knows about my heart condition), but when he saw me he was really relieved and gave me a hug. The look on his face said it all, and he invited me to have lunch with him and Maria. The simple lunch never tasted so good, with a glass of his homemade wine and a piece of goat and sheep cheese that he brought back from his trip to Italy. It was a joy, Padre!"

"That simple lunch was what friendship is all about. You experienced it, and your heart was full of love for him and Maria. That's life at its best!"

"Is that what our fellow Italians call 'la dolce vita'?"

"In the best sense of the phrase."

"I understand that perfectly. The connection with the life force is so strong that one knows—eureka! That's it, isn't it? That's the secret of life, isn't it? That's what everyone is after, isn't it—that mysterious connection with life?"

"You've got it, my good friend. That's the secret. Life is all about making this connection, and friendship is one of the best and most satisfying ways to make it. That's why friendships are so hard to make. They connect one soul to soul, and this is a sacred connection. Which is why friendships are so special, and why it

hurts so much when friendships are betrayed—as you and Penny know very well."

"Let's keep that for my creative writing, shall we?"

"By all means. Now, are you feeling better?"

"Yes. I get the point: jump in! Okay, I'm going to call up my book *The Sum of All Spiritual Paths* and do some editing. I have to get this one out while I'm working on my book of short stories. So, thank you Padre; and with this we can call it a day. Until we talk again..."

♥

About the Author

Orest Stocco was born in Calabria, Italy. He emmigrated to Canada and studied philosophy at university. A student of Gurdjieff's teaching for many years, his passion for writing inspired such works as *The Lion that Swallowed Hemingway* and *Healing with Padre Pio*. He lives in Georgian Bay, Ontario with his life mate Penny Lynn Cates. His personal dictum is: Life is an individual journey.

Visit him at: http://ostocco.wix.com/ostocco

Spiritual Musings Blog:

http://www.spiritualmusingsbyoreststocco.blogspot.com

ME AND MY SISPHYEAN ROCK